PRAISE FOR
WHY INFORMATION GROWS

Finalist for the 2015 Hayek Book and Lecture Prize

"Contains some innovative thinking about what drives growth that could help us to navigate the turbulence of the ever-more interconnected global economy." —*Nature*

"A mind-stretching, unconventional book that draws on information theory, physics, sociology, and economics to explain economic growth and why it occurs in some places [and] not all."
—*Pittsburgh Tribune-Review*

"Hidalgo invites us to understand the economy in an entirely different way. . . . A novel, holistic take on the dismal science." —*Kirkus Reviews*

"Anybody interested in the future of mathematical theory in economics should read César Hidalgo's book *Why Information Grows*. There are many things to like about this lucid account of the evolution of our scientific understanding of information. One of the most important may be the simplest. It illustrates what it means to think like a physicist."

—Paul Romer, founding director of the
NYU Stern Urbanization Project

"*Why Information Grows* shows us how humans infuse information into matter, making it more valuable than gold. Hidalgo's work brilliantly spotlights the true alchemy of the twenty-first century and its impact from economic complexity to national competitiveness."

—Albert-Laszlo Barabasi, distinguished professor and
director of Northeastern University's Center for
Complex Network Research and author of *Linked*

"This beautifully written and carefully researched book may set in motion a paradigm shift in economic thinking. Blending deep theory with detailed data, Hidalgo demonstrates that countries grow, firms prosper, and individuals thrive when they enmesh themselves in diverse, talented networks that produce complex physical order, i.e., information. Why do economies grow? Because information does."

—Scott Page, professor of complex systems,
political science, and economics at the University
of Michigan and author of *The Difference*

"The diverse set of perspectives that César Hidalgo brings to the eternal question of growth—from economic development theories to big data mining engines to elegantly crafted visualizations—underlies the central thesis of *Why Information Grows*: diversity. Including many diverse perspectives will ultimately create maximum complexity and chaos, which ultimately creates growth. Hidalgo makes a powerful case for the importance of creativity and imagination in our society's ability to make information—and economies—grow."

—John Maeda, partner, Kleiner Perkins Caufield & Byers,
and author of *The Laws of Simplicity*

Why Information Grows

The Evolution of Order, from Atoms to Economies

CÉSAR HIDALGO

BASIC BOOKS
New York

Published by Basic Books, an imprint of Perseus Books, LLC, a subsidiary
of Hachette Book Group, Inc.
Paperback first published in 2016 by Basic Books

Books published by Basic Books are available at special discounts for bulk
purchases in the United States by corporations, institutions, and other
organizations. For more information, please contact the Special Markets
Department at the Perseus Books Group, 2300 Chestnut Street, Suite 200,
Philadelphia, PA 19103, or call (800) 810-4145, ext. 5000, or e-mail special
.markets@perseusbooks.com.

Designed by Timm Bryson

Library of Congress Cataloging-in-Publication Data
Hidalgo, César A., 1979–
  Why information grows : the evolution of order, from atoms to
economies / Cesar Hidalgo.
    pages cm
  Includes bibliographical references and index.
  ISBN 978-0-465-04899-1 (hardback)—ISBN 978-0-465-03971-5 (e-book)
  1. Information theory in economics. 2. New products. 3. Economic
development. 4. Knowledge, Theory of—Economic aspects. 5. Physics. I.
Title.
  HB133.H6253 2015
  330.01'154—dc23

ISBN: 978-0-465-09684-8 (paperback)
                                                          2015000882

10 9 8 7 6 5 4 3 2 1

To Iris, Anna, and Mridu

CONTENTS

Prologue: The Eternal War   *ix*

Introduction: From Atoms to People to Economies   *xi*

PART I

Bits in Atoms   1

Chapter 1   The Secret to Time Travel   3

Chapter 2   The Body of the Meaningless   11

Chapter 3   The Eternal Anomaly   25

PART II

Crystallized Imagination   43

Chapter 4   Out of Our Heads!   49

Chapter 5   Amplifiers   65

PART III

The Quantization of Knowhow   73

Chapter 6   This Time, It's Personal   77

Chapter 7   Links Are Not Free   87

Chapter 8   In Links We Trust   109

Prologue: The Eternal War

PART IV

The Complexity of the Economy 127

Chapter 9 The Evolution of Economic Complexity 129
Chapter 10 The Sixth Substance 145
Chapter 11 The Marriage of Knowledge, Knowhow,
and Information 165

PART V

Epilogue 173

Chapter 12 The Evolution of Physical Order,
from Atoms to Economies 175

Acknowledgments: Bleeding Words 183
Notes 193
Index 219

PROLOGUE: THE ETERNAL WAR

The universe is made of energy, matter, and information, but information is what makes the universe interesting. Without information, the universe would be an amorphous soup. It would lack the shapes, structures, aperiodic orders, and fractal arrangements that give the universe both its beauty and its complexity.

Yet information is rare. It hides in pockets as it battles the universe's perennial march to disorder: the growth of entropy. This book is about the growth of information, and about the mechanisms that allow information to battle randomness and grow. These mechanisms include the natural processes that allow information to emerge and the social and economic mechanisms that contribute to the accelerating growth of information in society. This book is about the growth of information—the growth of physical order—that makes our planet unique, rich, and uneven, from atoms to economies.

Much of this book will focus on our planet and our species. This is because, from a cosmic perspective, our planet is a special place. We know of many places in our universe that concentrate more matter and energy than the Earth, but not of places that concentrate more information. Neutron stars are so dense that a spoonful of them weighs more than the Empire State Building. Black holes are so massive that they twist the geometry of space. Energy is also extremely abundant in the billions of stars that populate our galaxy, but not so much in our planet. So what makes our planet special is not that it is a singularity of matter or energy, but that it is a singularity of physical order, or information. Our planet is to information what a black hole is to matter and what a star is to energy. Our planet is where information lives, grows, and hides in an otherwise mostly barren universe.

But where does information come from? Why is information concentrated in our planet, and how is the growth of information facilitated by life? What are the social and economic mechanisms that enable information to continue growing in society? How does the social accumulation of information improve our capacity to accumulate even more information? And how do the mechanisms that contribute to the growth of information contribute to the social and economic unevenness of the global economy?

In the following pages, we will learn what information is, where it comes from, and why it grows. We will learn about the natural, social, and economic mechanisms that help information rebel against entropy. We will learn about the mechanisms that help information win small battles, prevailing stoically in our universe's only true war: the war between order and disorder; between entropy and information.

INTRODUCTION: FROM ATOMS
TO PEOPLE TO ECONOMIES

Ludwig was an unhappy man. Did the death of his son push him over the edge? Or was he broken down by his colleagues' criticisms? Maybe he loved atoms too much?

While on summer vacation, Ludwig killed himself. Elsa, his youngest daughter, found him dangling from a rope. She refused to talk about this episode throughout her life.

Of course, the Ludwig that I am talking about is Ludwig Boltzmann. Ludwig was a successful scientist, but also an insecure man. Ludwig made important contributions to our understanding of nature. His scientific contributions, however, did not go unchallenged.

Ludwig believed in atoms at a time when many of his colleagues considered atoms to be nothing more than a convenient analogy. Their skepticism troubled him. On the one hand, he knew he was on the right track. He had shown that the empirical behavior of gases could be attributed to the collective motion of molecules, or atoms. This finding gave him indirect evidence of the existence of atoms, but no way to observe these directly.

The lack of direct evidence left Ludwig vulnerable to the critiques of his colleagues. His nemesis, the physicist turned philosopher Ernst Mach, maintained that science should focus only on relationships among directly observable quantities. Additional theoretical constructs, like Boltzmann's atoms, were not allowed.

But Ludwig's troubles were not just social. For decades he had been trying to explain the origins of physical order. His attempts, while scientifically fruitful, were also unsuccessful. Ludwig's theory predicted the opposite of what he wanted to show. His everyday experience indicated that order was increasing all around him: flowers bloomed, trees sprouted, and the rapidly industrializing society mass-produced new gadgets every day. Ludwig's theory, however, predicted that order should not grow but disappear. It explained why heat flows from hot to cold, why swirls of milk disappear in coffee, and why whispers vanish in the wind. Ludwig showed that the microstructures of the universe gnaw away order, making it ephemeral. But he understood that this was not the full story and that he was missing the mechanisms that helped information transcend.

The growth of order troubled Ludwig. It disturbed him in a way that only a scientist can understand. He knew that something was missing from his theory, but he was unable to identify what that was. At the dusk of life, Ludwig became tired of battling both people and nature. Using a rope, he decided to take matter into his own hands. What was left was a shell of atoms that began a steady but certain decay, just as his theory predicted.

✳   ✳   ✳

In 1906 Ludwig ended his life, but not the philosophical problems that troubled him. To explain the origins of physical order, Ludwig connected phenomena occurring at different spatial scales, mainly atoms and gases.[1] Although it makes sense today, in Ludwig's time working across spatial scales was a practice that violated an implicit contract among scientists. Many of Ludwig's colleagues saw science as a hierarchy of Russian nesting dolls, with new structures emerging at each level. In this hierarchy, transgressing boundaries was thought unnecessary. Economics did not need psychology, just as psychology did not need biology. Biology did not need chemistry, and chemistry did not need physics. Explaining gases in terms of atoms, although not as preposterous as explaining human behavior in terms of biology, was seen as a betrayal of this implicit deal. Boltzmann had "sinned" by trying to explain the macroscopic properties of gases in terms of the motion of atoms.

*   *   *

The twentieth century vindicated Ludwig's view of atoms, and to a lesser extent his passion for crossing academic boundaries. Quantum mechanics helped connect Ludwig's atoms with chemistry and material science. Molecular biology and biochemistry helped connect the biology of the cell with the chemical properties of the proteins that populate them. On a parallel front, biology romanced psychology, as Darwin's theory became a staple explanation of human behavior.[2] Yet not all of the cross-fertilization took place near known scientific boundaries. Amid these multidisciplinary tangos, there was one concept that was promiscuous enough to play the field. This was the idea of *information*.

Information was the object of Ludwig's fascination. It was the thing that eluded him and also the thing he sought tirelessly to explain: why order in the universe could deteriorate even as it grew on Earth.

As information continued to grow in the twentieth century, so did the academic efforts looking to understand it. This time, however, the study of information was inspired not by the beauty of nature but by the horrors of war. During the Second World War competing armies developed a need to communicate using secret codes. These codes motivated efforts to decode intercepted messages, jump-starting the mathematical study of information.

Encoding and decoding messages was a mathematical problem that was too interesting to be abandoned as the war dwindled.

Mathematicians continued to formalize the idea of information, but they framed their efforts in the context of communication technologies, transcending the efforts to decipher intercepted messages. The mathematicians who triumphed became known as the world's first information theorists or cyberneticists. These pioneers included Claude Shannon, Warren Weaver, Alan Turing, and Norbert Wiener.

In the 1950s and 1960s the idea of information took science by storm. Information was welcomed in all academic fields as a powerful concept that cut across scientific boundaries. Information was neither microscopic nor macroscopic.[3] It could be inscribed sparsely on clay tablets or packed densely in a strand of DNA. For many practical purposes, the scale at which information was embodied was not crucial. This scale independence made the idea of information attractive to academics from all fields, who adopted the concept and endowed it with their own disciplinary flavor.

Biologists embraced the idea of information as they explored how genes encoded inheritance. Engineers, inspired by the work of Shannon, designed transmitters and receivers as they wired the world with analog and digital networks. Computer scientists, psychologists, and linguists attempted to model the mind by building electronic thinking machines. As the twentieth century outgrew its atomic zeitgeist, information became the new ace in everyone's hand.

The idea of information also found its way into the social sciences, and in particular into economics. Friedrich Hayek, an Austrian economist and a contemporary of Shannon, argued famously that prices transmitted information about the supply of and demand for goods. This helped reveal the information needed for Smith's "invisible hand" to work. As Hayek wrote, "In a system in which the knowledge of the relevant facts is dispersed among many people, prices can act to coördinate the separate actions of different people."[4]

The idea of information also helped economists understand some important market failures. George Akerlof became famous by showing that markets could fail to operate when people had asymmetric information about the quality of the goods they wanted to exchange.[5] On a parallel front, Herbert Simon, a polymath who contributed to economics, organizational theory, and artificial intelligence, introduced the idea of bounded rationality, which focused on the behavior of economic actors who had limited information about the world.

As the twentieth century continued to roar, the idea of information grew in status to an idea of global importance. Yet as the idea of information became more popular, we slowly began to forget about the physicality of information that had troubled Boltzmann. The word *information* became a synonym for the ethereal, the unphysical, the digital, the weightless, the immaterial. But information *is* physical. It is as physical as Boltzmann's atoms or the energy they carry in their motion. Information is not tangible; it is not a solid or a fluid. It does not have its own particle either, but it is as physical as movement and temperature, which also do not have particles of their own. Information is incorporeal, but it is always physically embodied. Information is not a thing; rather, it is the arrangement of physical things. It is *physical order*, like what distinguishes different shuffles of a deck of cards. What is surprising to most people, however, is that information is meaningless, even though the meaningless nature of information, much like its physicality, is often misunderstood.

*   *   *

In 1949 Claude Shannon and Warren Weaver published a short book entitled *The Mathematical Theory of Communication*. In its first section, Weaver described the conceptual aspects of information. In the second section, Shannon described the mathematics of what we now know as information theory.

For information theory to be properly understood, Shannon and Weaver needed to detach the word *information* from its colloquial meaning. Weaver made this distinction early on his essay: "The word information, in this theory, is used in a special sense that must not be confused with its ordinary usage. In particular, information must not be confused with meaning."[6]

Shannon also made this point early in his section, albeit invoking engineering arguments instead of semantic distinctions: "The fundamental problem of communication is that of reproducing in one point either exactly or approximately a message selected at another point. Frequently, the messages have meaning. . . . These semantic aspects of communication [referring to the meaning of a message] are irrelevant to the engineering problem."[7]

But why were Shannon and Weaver so eager to divorce information from meaning? They needed to separate information from meaning for both technical and philosophical reasons. On the technical side, Shannon was interested in the construction of machines that could help communicate information regardless of the meaning of the message. Mixing information and meaning obfuscated the engineering problem. On the philosophical side, Shannon and Weaver understood that their use of the words *information* and *meaning* referred to concepts that were fundamentally different. Humans, and some machines, have the ability to interpret messages and infuse them with meaning. But what travels through the wires or electromagnetic waves is not that meaning. It is simpler. It is just information.

It is hard for us humans to separate information from meaning because we cannot help interpreting messages. We infuse messages with meaning automatically, fooling ourselves to believe that the meaning of a message is carried in the message. But it is not. This is only an illusion. Meaning is derived from context and prior knowledge. Meaning is the interpretation that a knowledge agent, such as a human, gives to a message, but it is different from the physical order that carries the message, and different from the message itself. Meaning emerges when a message reaches a life-form or a machine with the ability to process information; it is not carried in the blots of ink, sound waves, beams of light, or electric pulses that transmit information.

Think of the phrase "September 11." When I say that phrase, most Americans automatically think of the 2001 attack on the Twin Towers. Chileans usually think about the 1973 coup d'état. But maybe when I am saying "September 11" I am just telling my students that I will be back at MIT on that date. As you can see, the meaning of the message is something that you construct. It is not part of the message, even if it seems to be. Meaning is something that we attach seamlessly as we interpret messages, because humans cannot help interpreting incoming bursts of physical order. This seamlessness does not mean that meaning and information are the same.

To create machines that could transmit information regardless of the meaning of the message, Shannon needed a formula to estimate the minimum number of characters required to encode a message. Building on the work of Harry Nyquist and Ralph Hartley, Shannon estimated how much information was needed to transmit a message through a clean or noisy channel. He also estimated the economies of communication brought by correlations in the structure of messages—such as the fact that in English the letter t is more likely to precede h than q. Shannon's philosophical excursions put him on a mathematical path similar to the one traversed by Boltzmann. At the end of the path, Shannon found a basic formula for encoding an arbitrary message with maximum efficiency. This formula allowed anyone to embody information in a magnetic disk, electromagnetic waves, or ink and paper. Shannon's formula was identical to the one Boltzmann had put forth almost fifty years earlier.[8] This coincidence was not an accident.

⁕   ⁕   ⁕

The convergence of Shannon's formula with Boltzmann's points to the physical nature of information. That physical reality is critical to seeing how a study of atoms can help us understand the economy. For the most part, the natural sciences have focused on describing our universe from atoms to people, connecting the simplicity of the atom with the complexity of life.* The social sciences have focused on the links among people, society, and economies, recasting humans as a fundamental unit—a social and economic atom, if I may. Yet this divorce is not lossless, as the mechanisms that allow information to grow transcend the barriers that separate the lifeless from the living, the living from the social, and the social from the economic.

So I will dedicate the following pages to an exploration of the mechanisms that contribute to the growth of information at all scales, from atoms to economies. Not from atoms to people, or from people to economies, as it is usually done. This will help us create bridges between the physical, biological, social, and economic factors that contribute to the growth of information and also limit our capacity to process information. That information-processing capacity involves computation, and at the scale of humans it requires the "software" we know colloquially as *knowledge* and *knowhow*. The result will be a book about the history of our universe, centered not on the arrow of time but on the arrow of complexity.

And it is the arrow of complexity—the growth of information— that marks the history of our universe and species. Billions of years ago, soon after the Big Bang, our universe did not have the capacity to generate the order that made Boltzmann marvel and which we all take for granted. Since then, our universe has been marching toward disorder, as Boltzmann predicted, but it has also been busy producing pockets that concentrate enormous quantities of physical order, or information. Our planet is a chief example of such a pocket.

---

* The obvious exceptions to this are geology and astronomy.

The wave of stars that preceded the formation of our solar system synthesized the atomic elements needed for life to form. These elements included carbon, oxygen, calcium, nitrogen, and iron. From the corpses of these stellar ancestors a new generation of stars was formed. This time around, the planets that orbited them had the chemical richness required for life to evolve. Our planet, which is four to five billion years old, has since then exploited this chemical richness to become a singularity of complexity. For billions of years information has continued to grow in our planet: first in its chemistry, then in simple life-forms, more recently in us. In a universe characterized mostly by empty space, our planet is an oasis where information, knowledge, and knowhow continue to increase, powered by the sun but also by the self-reinforcing mechanisms that we know as life.

Yet the continuity between the physics of the stars and the life-forms that populate our planet includes just two stops along the timeline of complexity and information. The evolution of information cuts across all boundaries, extending even to the information begotten by our economy and society. Information, when understood in its broad meaning as physical order, is what our economy produces. It is the *only* thing we produce, whether we are biological cells or manufacturing plants. This is because information is not restricted to messages. It is inherent in all the physical objects we produce: bicycles, buildings, streetlamps, blenders, hair dryers, shoes, chandeliers, harvesting machines, and underwear are all made of information. This is not because they are made of ideas but because they embody physical order. Our world is pregnant with information. It is not an amorphous soup of atoms, but a neatly organized collection of structures, shapes, colors, and correlations. Such ordered structures are the manifestations of information, even when these chunks of physical order lack any meaning.

But begetting information is not easy. Our universe struggles to do so. Our ability to beget information, and to produce the items,

infrastructures, and institutions we associate with prosperity, requires us to battle the steady march toward disorder that char-
acterizes our universe and which troubled Boltzmann. To battle
disorder and allow information to grow, our universe has a few
tricks up its sleeve. These tricks involve out-of-equilibrium systems, the accumulation of information in solids, and the ability of
matter to compute. Together these three mechanisms contribute
to the growth of information in small islands or pockets where
information can grow and hide, like our body or our planet.

So it is the accumulation of information and of our ability to
process information that defines the arrow of growth encom-
passing the physical, the biological, the social, and the economic,
and which extends from the origin of the universe to our modern
economy. It is the growth of information that unifies the emergence of life with the growth of economies, and the emergence of
complexity with the origins of wealth.

Yet the growth of information is uneven, not just in the universe
but on our planet. It takes places in pockets with the capacity to
beget and store information. Cities, firms, and teams are the embodiment of the pockets where our species accumulates the capacity to produce information. Of course, the capacity of these cities,
firms, and teams to beget information is highly uneven. Some are
able to produce packets of information that embody concepts begotten by science fiction. Others are not quite there.

So by asking what information is and why it grows, we will be
exploring not only the evolution of physical order but that of economic order as well. We will be connecting basic physical principles with information theory, and also with theories of social
capital, economic sociology, theories of knowledge, and the empirics of industrial diversification and economic development. By asking why information grows, we will be asking about the evolution
of prosperity, about rich and poor nations, about productive and
unproductive teams, about the role of institutions in our capacity

to accumulate knowledge, and about the mechanisms that limit people's capacity to produce packets of physically embodied information. We will be taking a step back from traditional approaches to understanding social and economic phenomena. Instead, we will be generating a description that seeks to integrate physical, biological, social, and economic mechanisms to help explain the continuous growth of something that is not a *thing*. That something, which fascinates you and me as much as it did Boltzmann, is physical order, or information. It is the high concentration of complexity that we see every time we open our eyes, not because information is everywhere in the universe but because we are born from it, and it is born from us.

PART I

Bits in Atoms

1

The Secret to Time Travel

The chair where I waited for my daughter's delivery was not that comfortable. My wife, Anna, and I had arrived at the Massachusetts General Hospital at 6:30 p.m. that Saturday. We had stayed at home waiting for her contractions to evolve and decided to hit the hospital when they were only a few minutes apart. Her contractions intensified when she was in triage, but the epidural she received a couple of hours later brought her the numbness she needed to rest. It was now 2:00 a.m. The night was peaceful. All we could hear was the infrequent noise of the pump inflating her blood pressure monitor. The room was lit by a few displays and by the streetlights bouncing off the Charles River. In that dim light all I could see was Anna resting peacefully in her bed. I held her hand as I waited for the delivery of our daughter in an armchair that, as I told you, was not that comfortable.

At 3:00 a.m. the nurse told us that it was time for Anna to start pushing. Anna was fully dilated, and Iris—our daughter— was making one of the most important trips of her life. It took only twenty-six minutes for Anna to push Iris into the hands of the nervous but focused medical student who received her. Twenty-six minutes sounds like a short time for delivery, and it is. Yet I will argue that the trip that Iris made that night was not a twenty-six-minute trip down a few inches of birth canal but a hundred-thousand-year journey from a distant past to an alien future. In twenty-six minutes Iris traveled from the ancientness of her mother's womb to the modernity of twenty-first-century society. Birth is, in essence, time travel.

Up until that night, with the exception of a few sounds, Iris had experienced a world that was no different from the one experienced by babies one hundred thousand years ago. She had been carried inside her mother's womb hearing mostly the voices of her parents, oblivious to the complexity of the modern world that swirled around her. That obliviousness changed that night.

Iris was born at 3:26 a.m. in a room that was illuminated not by sunbeams but by fluorescent and incandescent bulbs. Her paternal grandparents, who were anxiously waiting to hear about her delivery, saw her face for the first time in an email attachment. The music that filled the delivery room minutes after Iris was born came not from the birds or the trees but from the speakers of a tablet computer that obeyed the orders of an algorithm that chose a song for us.* Iris' trip that night was only a few inches long and lasted a few minutes, but in a deep sense it was a much longer journey. That night, she traveled from a distant past into a present that was literally fantastic.

Although Iris' trip is special to me, her form of time travel is not uncommon. Being born in the twenty-first century is an alien experience for most babies. The twenty-first century is a world quite different from the one where our species evolved. It is a surreal world populated by tangible objects that were dreamed before they were constructed. The delivery room where Iris made her journey was full of tangible objects, but those objects, per se, were not what made the world she found modern. The difference

---

* The song was "Raindrops," by Cillo. It played in Pandora, and I thumbed up the song that night.

between the world where Iris was born and the world of early hominids resides not in the physicality of matter but in the way in which matter is arranged. That physical order is information. Iris' nighttime delivery was facilitated not by objects, but by the information embodied in these objects and by the practical uses of knowledge and knowhow that these objects implicitly carry. Her nighttime delivery was illuminated not just by light bulbs but by the understanding of electricity, energy, and materials embodied in those light bulbs. Iris was kept warm that night not by a random collection of threads but by blankets that wove together matter, knowledge, and imagination. Paradoxically, Iris was born into a nonfictional world that, although tangible, is made of fiction. This world is different from the one in which our species evolved only in the way in which matter is arranged.

The fact that objects embody information and imagination may seem obvious. Information is a fundamental aspect of nature, one that is older than life itself. It is also an aspect of nature that accelerated with life. Consider the replication of information-rich molecules, such as DNA and RNA. The replication of DNA and RNA is not the replication of matter but the replication of the information that is embodied in matter. Living organisms are highly organized structures that process and produce information. Yet, our focus here will not be on the information-generating capacity that is embodied in the intimacy of our cells but that which emerged with humans and society. Humans are special animals when it comes to information, because unlike other species, we have developed an enormous ability to encode large volumes of information outside our bodies. Naively, we can think of this information as the information we encode in books, sheet music, audio recordings, and video. Yet for longer than we have been able to write we have been embodying information in artifacts or objects, from arrows to microwave ovens, from stone axes to the physical Internet. So our ability to produce chairs, computers, tablecloths, and wineglasses is a simple answer to the eternal question: what is the difference between us, humans, and all other species? The answer is that we are able to create physical instantiations of the objects we imagine, while other species are stuck with nature's inventory.[1]

In the next pages I will describe the physical, social, and economic mechanisms that explain the growth of information in our world and our universe. These are the mechanisms responsible for producing the physical order that made the destination of Iris' birth both tangible and magical. On the one hand, we will study the physics of information. This will explain what information is and the physical mechanisms that allow information to emerge. Yet the physics of information can explain only the simplest forms of physical order. To explain the order that pervades our modern society, we will need to go beyond physics and explore the social and economic processes that allow groups of people to produce information. These processes involve the formation of the social and professional networks in which the capacity to socially process information resides. This capacity involves the accumulation of knowledge and knowhow.

Knowledge and knowhow are two fundamental capacities that relate to computation, and both are crucial for the accumulation of information in the economy and society. Yet knowledge and knowhow are not the same. Simply put, knowledge involves relationships or linkages between entities. These relationships are often used to predict the outcomes of events without having to act them out.[2] For instance, we know that tobacco use increases the likelihood of lung cancer, and we can use that linkage to anticipate the consequences of tobacco use without the need to use tobacco ourselves.

Knowhow is different from knowledge because it involves the capacity to perform actions, which is tacit.[3] For example, most of us know how to walk, even though we do not know how we walk.

Most of us know how to identify and label objects in an image, even though we do not know how we accomplish those perceptual and verbal tasks. Most of us know how to recognize objects from different angles, identify faces, digest food, and recognize emotions, even though we cannot explain how we do it. We can do these tasks, however, because we have knowhow. Knowhow is the tacit computational capacity that allows us to perform actions, and it is accumulated at both the individual and collective levels.

The tacit nature of knowhow seems strange, as it makes us feel like automatons that are unaware of what we are doing. Yet there is nothing strange in that. As Marvin Minsky, one of the fathers of artificial intelligence, once said: "No computer has ever been designed that is ever aware of what it's doing; but most of the time, we aren't either."[4]

Another distinction that I should mention up front is the one between information *as* something and information *about* something, such as the information we transmit in a message. Think of a car. I can tell you that my car is red and has a six-speed manual transmission and a 1.6 liter engine. This is all information about my car, but it is not the information that my car is. As we will learn in the next chapters, my car is made of information that is not about something. This is physical order.

For the most part, I will use the word *information* to indicate physical order, like that embodied in objects; I will go into the weeds of this definition in the next chapter. I use this definition because it helps me construct a simpler theory of the growth of information, in which physical order, regardless of whether or not it was produced to convey meaning, coevolves with the universe's ability to compute. In a social and economic context this computational capacity involves both knowledge and knowhow.

So to explain the growth of information in nature and society we will explore the coevolution of physical order and the knowledge and knowhow that allow our universe to beget that physical order. This will bring us from the simplest physical systems, where information emerges spontaneously, to the complexity of our society, where large accumulations of knowledge and knowhow are needed for information to continue to grow.

The case of society and economies is the one that is most complex, as here the accumulation of knowledge and knowhow becomes highly constrained. Much like information, which is embodied in objects, knowledge and knowhow always need to be physically embodied. Yet unlike information, knowledge and knowhow are embodied in humans and networks of humans that have a finite capacity to embody knowledge and knowhow. The finiteness of humans and of the networks we form limits our ability to accumulate and transmit knowledge and knowhow, leading to spatial accumulations of knowledge and knowhow that result in global inequality. So the need for knowledge and knowhow to be embodied in humans and networks of humans can help explain the unevenness of our world. These are ideas that I will cover in Parts III and IV and which I will validate using data on the products produced by groups of people in different locations, since products—which are made of information—are expressions of the knowledge and knowhow that are available in a location.

So the central actors that I will use to describe the growth of information in our planet include physical objects, as the physical embodiment of information, and people, as the fundamental embodiment of knowledge and knowhow. From this fundamental perspective we will describe the economy as the system by which people accumulate knowledge and knowhow to create packets of physical order, or products, that augment our capacity to accumulate more knowledge and knowhow and, in turn, accumulate more information. We will focus largely on the growth of information, knowledge, and knowhow in the economy by first creating a theory of products in terms of physical order and then explaining the social and economic mechanisms that enable our society to accumulate the knowledge and knowhow we need to produce products.

Before we go there, however, I need to make sure we have a common understanding of the fundamental physics of information and its non-obvious origins. I will start by explaining what information is both mathematically and physically. As we will see, this will help us understand why Boltzmann and Shannon both bumped into the same formula; it will also teach us about the fundamental physical principles that allow information to grow.

2

The Body of the Meaningless

Suppose that we were asked to arrange the following into categories—distance, mass, electric force, entropy, beauty, melody. I think there are the strongest grounds for placing entropy alongside beauty and melody, and not with the first three. Entropy is only found when the parts are viewed in association, and it is by viewing or hearing the parts in association that beauty and melody are discerned.

—ARTHUR EDDINGTON

To invent, you need a good imagination and a pile of junk.

—THOMAS A. EDISON

A few months ago an article on the front page of a Chilean newspaper's business section caught my eye. The article talked about a Chilean who had bought the world's most expensive car. The car, a Bugatti Veyron, had a sticker price of more than $2.5 million, and its purchase represented one of the most flamboyant acts of conspicuous consumption I have ever seen.

After a quick Web search I estimated the per-kilo price of the car, which turned out to be roughly $1,300 (or about $600 a pound).[1] To put this price in context, we can look at the per-kilo price of gold and silver. Depending on the day, the price of a kilo of pure silver is about $1,000, while that of a kilo of gold is around $50,000.[2] For comparison, consider that the per-kilo price of a regular car ranges from $10 for a Hyundai Accent to $60 for a top-of-the-line BMW such as the M6. So although the Bugatti is not worth its weight in gold, it is worth more than its weight in silver, and a Hyundai accent is worth at least its weight in bronze.

Now, you may argue that comparing a kilo of Bugatti and a kilo of silver is pure nonsense, since there is not much you can do with an actual kilo of Bugatti. Yet this nonsense has much to teach us about how physical order, or information, is packed into a product.

Imagine for a second that you just won a Bugatti Veyron in the lottery. Pumped up, you decide to take your new car for a drive. In your excitement, you crash the Bugatti into a wall, escaping unharmed but a little sad, since you did not have any car insurance. The car is a total wreck. Now, how much is that kilo of Bugatti worth?

The answer to this question is perfectly obvious. The dollar value of the car evaporated in the seconds it took you to crash it against that wall, but its weight did not. So where did the value go? The car's dollar value evaporated in the crash not because the crash destroyed the atoms that made up the Bugatti but because the crash changed the way in which these were arranged. As the parts that made the Bugatti were pulled apart and twisted, the information that was embodied in the Bugatti was largely destroyed. This is another way of saying that the $2.5 million worth of value was stored not in the car's atoms but in the way those atoms were arranged.[3] That arrangement is information.[4]

So the value of the Bugatti is connected to physical order, which is information, even though people still debate what information is.[5] According to Claude Shannon, the father of information theory, information is a measure of the minimum volume of communication required to uniquely specify a message. That is, it's the number of bits we need to communicate an arrangement, like the arrangement of atoms that made the Bugatti.

To grasp Shannon's definition of information firmly, however, it is better to start with something simpler than a Bugatti. Here I will use a tweet. A tweet is a message of 140 characters used in the microbroadcasting platform known as Twitter. A tweet, like a Bugatti, is a little packet of information, but unlike the Bugatti, we create it as an act of communication. For the purposes of Shannon's theory, however, that doesn't matter. According to Shannon, information is the minimum volume of data we need to specify a message, any message. Whether this message is a tweet made of random characters or the wittiest tweet you ever saw is irrelevant from the perspective of Shannon's information theory.

So how much information is contained in a tweet? To put a number on a tweet's information content, consider a hypothetical game played by two Twitter users, Abby and Brian. In this game, Abby and Brian have to guess each other's tweets using only yes-or-no questions. To play the game they have a book that contains every possible tweet that could be ever tweeted. The game starts when Abby randomly chooses a tweet from her book. Then she asks Brian to guess her tweet using only yes-or-no questions. What Shannon teaches us is that the amount of information that is embodied in a tweet is equal to the minimum number of yes-or-no questions that Brian needs to ask to guess Abby's tweet with 100 percent accuracy.[6] But how many questions is that?

For simplicity, we will assume that Abby and Brian are using an "alphabet" of thirty-two characters: the lowercase English alphabet plus a few extra characters, such as the space ( ), the slash (/), the comma (,), the period (.), and of course the at symbol (@) and the hash (#). Also, without any loss of generality, we will assume that Abby and Brian have tables mapping each character to a number (a = 1, b = 2, [. . .], @ = 31, # = 32).

The best way for Brian to guess Abby's tweet is to use each question to divide the search space of possible tweets in half. Brian can do this by guessing Abby's tweet character by character. If Brian decides to use this strategy, his first yes-or-no question should be "Is the first character larger than 16?" If Abby answers no, then Brian will know that the first character in Abby's tweet is between the letters *a* and *p*. With that information in mind, Brian should ask a second question that splits in half the set of remaining characters: "Is the first character larger than 8?" If Abby says yes, Brian will know that the first character of Abby's tweet is between character 9 and character 16 (between the letters *i* and *p*). Now, you should be able to guess what Brian's next question will be: "Is the first character larger than 12?"

With each question Brian is cutting the number of possible characters in half. Since there are thirty-two possible characters, Brian will need only five questions to guess each character (you need to divide 32 by 2 five times to cut down the set of options to just one). Finally, since there are 140 characters in a tweet, Brian will need 140 × 5 = 700 yes-or-no questions, or bits, to uniquely identify Abby's tweet.[7]

Shannon's theory tells us that we need 700 bits, or yes-or-no questions, to communicate a tweet written using a thirty-two-character alphabet. Shannon's theory is also the basis of modern communication systems. By quantifying the number of bits we need to encode messages, he helped develop digital communication technologies. Yet what Shannon did not know when he developed his formula was that it was identical to the formula discovered by Boltzmann nearly half a century earlier. At the suggestion of John von Neumann, the famous Hungarian mathematician, Shannon decided to call his measure "entropy," since Shannon's formula was equivalent to the formula for entropy used by statistical physicists.

(Also—as the legend goes—von Neumann told Shannon that calling his measure entropy would guarantee Shannon's victory in every argument, since nobody really knew what entropy was.)

But the interpretation of entropy and information that emerged from Shannon's work was hard to reconcile both with the traditional use of the word *information* and with the interpretation of entropy that emerged from Boltzmann's work. The clash between Shannon's use of the word *information* and the colloquial use of *information* that is still prevalent today is easy to understand using computers as an example. Think of your personal computer. Whether this is a desktop, laptop, or smartphone, you use that computer to store pictures, documents, and software. You refer to these pictures and documents as "information" and of course are well aware that this information is stored in your device's hard drive. Yet, according to Shannon, if we were to flip all of the bits of the hard drive randomly, effectively deleting all of your pictures and documents, we would be increasing the amount of information embodied in the hard drive. How can that be? Well, Shannon's definition of information counts only the number of bits needed to communicate the state of a system (in this case, the sequence of bits stored in your hard drive). Since we need more bits to communicate the state of a hard drive full of random data than that of a hard drive containing pictures and documents, which include correlations that make the sequence compressible, Shannon's definition concludes that there is more information stored in your hard drive after we flipped bits randomly. Technically, Shannon is correct to say that we do need more bits to communicate the contents of a hard drive containing random data than of one containing pictures and documents. But Shannon's theory of information—which is effectively a theory of communication engineering—needs to be expanded to be reconciled with both the colloquial meaning of the word *information* and the work of Boltzmann. To complement Shannon's work I will need to first explain the definition of entropy that emerged from the work of Boltzmann and then advance a description that we can use to identify the information-rich states that we associate with a computer filled with pictures and documents.

To understand the difference between Boltzmann's and Shannon's definitions of entropy, consider a half-full stadium.* One important characteristic of a half-full stadium is that there are many ways in which the stadium can be half full, and by exploring those different ways we can explain what entropy is.

First we will consider the case in which people can move throughout the stadium with no restrictions. Here, one way for the stadium to be half full is to have everyone sitting as close to the field as possible, leaving all upper seats vacant. Another way is to have everyone sitting as far from the field as possible (leaving all lower seats vacant). Yet people can also fill up half of a stadium by occupying a random set of all seats.

Now, to use the stadium example to explain entropy I need to introduce two more ideas. First I will call each configuration of people sitting in a stadium a *state* of the system (or technically a *microstate*). Second, I will assume that we can identify equivalent configurations using some criterion that—for the purposes of this illustration—can be as simple as the average row being occupied.

In this example, the statistical-physics definition of entropy is simply the fraction of all states that are equivalent (it's actually the logarithm of the fraction, but this technicality is irrelevant for the point I am trying to make). So entropy is lowest when people are sitting as close to the field as possible or as far away as possible, since there is only one way for people to be sitting as close to (or far from) to the field as possible.[8] Entropy is largest when

---

* Mathematical geeks who might get too picky should consider a stadium in which the number of rows does not increase as we get farther from the field and where the number of a row indicates the distance between a seat in that row and the field.

the average row being occupied is the center row, since there are many ways in which we could arrange people in seats so that the average row that is being occupied is exactly the one in the middle. In Boltzmann's definition of entropy, entropy is the multiplicity of equivalent states; in the case of the stadium, the largest number of equivalent states exists when the average row that is being occupied is the center one.

It is worth noting that entropy, even though commonly associated with disorder, is not exactly a measure of disorder. Entropy measures the multiplicity of a state (the number of states that are equivalent). It so happens, however, that disordered states tend to have high multiplicity, so in practice high-entropy states are extremely likely to be disordered. That is why equating disorder with entropy is not such a bad simplification. Yet entropy can increase without increasing disorder. Consider the expansion of gas in a box that doubles in size (or the expansion of people in a stadium that doubles in size). The entropy of the gas increases with the size of the box because there are more ways in which we can arrange the gas particles in a larger box. Yet the gas in the larger box is not more disordered than the one in the smaller box.

Shannon was concerned with communicating the microstate of a system, such as an individual tweet or the arrangement of people sitting in our hypothetical stadium, so he equated information with entropy (often using those words as synonyms). Communicating one of the microstates in which the average row being occupied is the center row requires more bits because for that condition there are many microstates that are equivalent, so we need a very specific message to identify which microstate is the one we want to communicate. So in Shannon's language, information and entropy are functionally equivalent because the number of bits you need to specify a message (Shannon's information) is a function of the number of possible messages that could be transmitted (the multiplicity of states, which we know as entropy). Yet this does not make entropy and information the same thing. As Manfred Eigen, the winner of the 1967 Nobel Prize in Chemistry, remarked: "Entropy refers to an average of (physical) states, information to a particular (physical) state."[9]

But the fact that we need more bits to communicate a state in which everyone has randomly chosen a seat in the stadium or in which the bits in a hard drive have been randomly flipped does not mean that these are states that embody more order or information. Information involves an increasing number of bits, but it is more than that. In the stadium example the myriad of states that involve people picking a seat randomly is characterized by the highest amount of entropy but the lowest amount of order (even though some of these states might be highly ordered). In fact, in the natural sciences, and among the general public, there has been a long tradition of equating information with something more than bits, something that involves order. Think of geneticists talking about the information contained in DNA, or about the information contained in music scores, a reel of film, or a book. In these examples the word *information* refers to the presence of order, not just the number of bits needed to communicate a genetic sequence, book, or music score.

But ordered states are both uncommon and peculiar. First I will explain what I mean by "uncommon" in this context. Next I will explain the peculiarity of information-rich states, which involves the correlations that give the word *information* its widespread colloquial meaning.

To explain the uncommonality of ordered states, let me extend the stadium example to something closer to what Boltzmann described in the context of atoms. Consider now that the stadium is half full, but also that people are not allowed to move unrestrictedly. Now the only states that are allowed are those in which the average row being occupied is the center row. In the case of a physical system, this is equivalent to fixing the energy of the system. Yet since there are many different states in which the average row occupied is the center row, the system still has many states to choose from. Most of these states are quite random. Others, however, are quite peculiar. People in a stadium can act like pixels in a screen, so some of these states include people sitting in arrangements that spell words, such as INFORMATION, or that result in drawings, such as the face of Hello Kitty. But how common are these peculiar states?

To identify which states are common, we need a method to map out the set of all possible states. One way to achieve this is to look at how these states are connected. We can say that two states are connected if I can get from one to the other with a simple transformation. For simplicity, let's consider all transformations in which everyone is allowed to move to a neighboring seat, as long as the new state is also a state that satisfies our average middle row constraint. These transformations include everyone moving one seat to the right and also the transformation in which a person in the bottom half of the stadium moves up one seat when a person on the top half of the stadium moves down one seat.

In principle, we can use these transformations to reach any allowed state. In practice, however, reaching any state is not that easy. If we let the people in the stadium evolve their seating arrangements by choosing a neighboring seat at random (and, of course, allowing only transformations that satisfy our middle row constraint), we will never bump into the states that spell words or draw pictures. These states are extremely uncommon and hard to reach. This exercise helps illustrate the definition of information that involves order. In a physical system, information is the opposite of entropy, as it involves uncommon and highly correlated configurations that are difficult to arrive at.

Uncommon configurations of atoms, like a Bugatti or a guitar, embody more information than more common configurations of the same atoms, even though technically (and Shannon is right about this) communicating an ordered configuration and communicating a disordered configuration require the same amount of bits if we ignore the correlations that are prevalent in an ordered state (which we can use to compress the sequence and hence reduce the number of bits we need to communicate the ordered state). Yet despite the differences in interpretation that mire down the reconciliation of Shannon's and Boltzmann's ideas, we can still conclude that not only are messages made of information, but most things are.

So let's get back to the Bugatti. The case of the Bugatti is not as simple as that of a tweet because it involves positioning gazillions of atoms and not just 140 characters. Also, as I just described, the case of the Bugatti is not one in which we are searching for any possible configuration of atoms; rather, we are searching for configurations that produce something that is like a Bugatti (like the example of rare seating arrangements in the stadium). For instance, rotating the tires of the Bugatti results in exchanges of atoms that do not change any of the fundamental properties that we are interested in, so we consider all of the Bugattis with rotated tires to be equivalent. The group of Bugattis in perfect shape, however, is relatively small, meaning that in the set of all possible rearrangement of atoms—like people moving in a stadium—very few of these involve a Bugatti in perfect condition. The group of Bugatti wrecks, on the other hand, is a configuration with a higher multiplicity of states (higher entropy), and hence a configuration that embodies less information (even though each of these states requires more bits to be communicated). Yet the largest group of all, the one that is equivalent to people sitting randomly in the stadium, is the one describing Bugattis in their "natural" state. This is the state where iron is a mineral ore and aluminum is embedded in bauxite. The destruction of the Bugatti, therefore, is the destruction of information. The creation of the Bugatti, on the other hand, is the embodiment of information.

The stadium example helps us understand that the configurations of matter that embody information, such as the Bugatti, are
uncommon and hard to reach. The stadium example also stresses
the dynamic origins of order, since for any form of order to come
about atoms need to find their right place. The problem is that
systems are not free to jump from any state to any state. As the
stadium example illustrated, the present state of a system constrains the possible paths that a system can take, and for a system
to travel from disorder to order, many consecutive moves need to
be made. Unfortunately, there are fewer paths leading a system
from disorder to order than from order to disorder. In a system
whose evolution is affected by chance (like in a statistical physics
system), getting a series of consecutive moves right is not easy.

Think of a Rubik's cube. A Rubik's cube illustrates the connection between available paths and entropy perfectly, since you will
never be able to solve a Rubik's cube by chance (even though in
your desperation you might try). A Rubik cube has more than 43
quintillion possible states (that is, 43,252,003,274,489,856,000, or
4.3×10^{19}), only one of which is perfectly ordered. Also, a Rubik's
cube is a system in which order is not that far away, since it is
always possible to solve a Rubik's cube in twenty moves or less.[10]
That sounds like a relatively small number, but finding the right
twenty moves is not an easy feat. Most people solve the cube by
traversing paths that are much more circuitous. The basic method
for solving the cube (building the top cross, positioning the cor-
ners, completing the middle row, etc.) usually takes more than
fifty moves to complete (and until recently people believed that
the number of moves needed to solve the cube was larger than
twenty).[11] This goes to show that in a Rubik's cube there are only
a few paths that lead to the perfectly ordered solution, and these
paths, whether short or long, are rare, as they are hidden among
the immense number of paths that push the cube away from order.
So the growth of entropy is like a Rubik's cube in the hands of a

child. In nature information is rare not only because information-rich states are uncommon but also because they are inaccessible given the way in which nature explores the possible states.

But what are the properties of information-rich states? And how can we use knowledge about their properties to identify them? One important characteristic of information-rich states is that these involve both long-range and short-range correlations. In the case of the Rubik's cube these correlations are conspicuous[12]: when the cube is perfectly ordered, each color is surrounded by as many neighbors of the same color as it possibly can be. Yet correlations are conspicuous not only in man-made objects, like a Rubik's cube, but also in nature. Consider a strand of DNA, which involves a long sequence of nucleotides (A, C, T, and G). Strands of DNA are very long, and despite great scientific advances we still do not know what most DNA sequences do. Yet we can still identify portions of DNA that are rich in information. The simplest way to identify information is to compare a strand of DNA with a random sequence of nucleotides (a sequence in which A, C, T, and G are selected by throwing a four-faced die). By comparing a sequence of actual DNA and a random sequence, we can identify portions of DNA that are uncommon—meaning that they should not appear based on what we would expect from the random sequence. These uncommon sequences involve unexpected correlations between neighboring nucleotides (they "spell words"), as well as correlations between faraway nucleotides (they "spell paragraphs and chapters" and make "references" to "words" that have been used before). Ultimately, these correlations reveal the existence of information in DNA, as they tell us that the sequences found in DNA are not those that would be arrived at by exploring the space of sequences at random; rather, they are rare sequences that have been found, preserved, honed, and expanded through the iterative work of evolution.[13] Also, the DNA example tells us that the presence of information is independent from our ability to decode it. The order in DNA is not a reintroduction of meaning into the definition of information. We can detect the existence of information in DNA even though we are hard pressed to know what many of these sequences mean or do. So we are not confusing information with meaning, or looking for information that is in the eye of the beholder. The correlations that characterize the information we transmit through human forms of communication (such as English) or biological forms of communications (such as DNA) are there whether we know how to decode them or not. They are a characteristic of information-rich states, not of who is observing them. This tells us that when it comes to communication, the meaningful rides on the meaningless. Our ability to transmit meaningful messages builds on the prior existence of meaningless forms of physical order. These meaningless forms of order are what information truly is.*

Finally, I will connect the multiplicity-of-states definition of entropy with our ability to process information (that is, compute). As we saw in the Rubik's cube example, information-rich states are hard to find, not only because they are rare but also because there are few paths leading to them. That's why we equate the ability of someone to solve a Rubik's cube with a form of intelligence, since those who know how to solve a Rubik's cube get credit for finding these rare paths (or memorizing the rules to find them). But there are also examples simpler than a Rubik's cube that we can use to illustrate the connection between the multiplicity of states of a system and computation. Consider the game where babies put shapes such as cylinders and cubes in their respective holes. At fourteen months most babies are pretty good at putting balls and

---

* Of course, a perfectly correlated picture, such as one painted uniformly in one color (a giant red square), will also embody little information, as the correlations are so strong that we can predict the entire picture from one pixel. This tells us that information is contained not in perfectly ordered or disordered structures but in fractal-like, aperiodic, but somehow regular structures that embody correlations at many different distances, like those of a face, a tree, a car engine, or even a cloud.

cylinders into holes, but they struggle with cubes, squares, triangles, and other shapes.[14] Why? Putting a ball into a hole is easy because balls look the same no matter how you rotate them (all states are equivalent). Putting a cylinder in a hole is also easy because the cylinder does not change if you rotate it around its axis. Fitting a cube into a hole, however, is more difficult, since there are few rotations that work. The case of a triangle is even worse, since even fewer rotations fit. The case of a triangle with unequal sides (in which only one rotation works) is the baby equivalent of a Rubik's cube, since only a few babies are able to solve that. So as you can see, as babies develop the ability to fit shapes into holes, they are developing the ability to find these rare low-entropy states. Finding rare but useful states in a continuum of possible configurations is a good minimalistic model of our ability to process information, or compute. This applies to babies putting shapes into holes, or to teenagers solving Rubik's cubes.

✳   ✳   ✳

We started this chapter by wrecking an imaginary Bugatti to illustrate that physical order, or information, is what is embodied in a product. Yet we have not come close to explaining where that order comes from, why it grows, and why it has economic value. In the next chapter we will explore the origins of physical order from a fundamental perspective, leaving to later chapters the questions of what kind of order humans accumulate in an economy, why that order is useful, and how humans help order grow. After we are done creating a description of products in terms of information, we will describe the social and economic mechanisms that limit our ability to produce order, like the order that was embodied in the Bugatti. This will help us understand the evolution of our world's economic unevenness and extend our understanding of the growth of information to ideas of social and economic development.

3

The Eternal Anomaly

*The irreversibility of time is the mechanism that
brings order out of chaos.*
—ILYA PRIGOGINE

On occasion, we all have wanted to reverse time. Sometimes we
want to reverse time to avoid simple mistakes. Sometimes we want
to avoid big mistakes. But we all know that the size of the mistake
does not matter. Time flows in one direction: from past to present,
from young to old, from life to death.[1]

The irreversibility of time, much like the attraction of gravity,
is a physical reality so conspicuous that it seems it must have an
obvious explanation. But it does not. In fact, up until the twentieth
century, the irreversible march of time was a puzzle that left some
of the most brilliant minds of our species at a loss. Isaac Newton
and Albert Einstein both produced successful theories of motion,
which are technically time-reversible.[2] They explain the motion
of cannonballs, planets, and satellites without a clear distinction
between where an object is and where it is going. This symmetry,
which is true for simple systems, fails to explain why lions eat and
digest gazelles instead of regurgitating whole live animals, and

why crashed Bugattis do not self-assemble back into functioning vehicles.

Here we are interested in the irreversibility of time, not only because it is a fascinating natural puzzle but also because it is connected intimately with the physical origins of information. Both the irreversibility of time and the physical origins of information are characteristics of the universe that are not encoded in the laws of motion that govern the movement of single particles, whether those laws are Newton's or Einstein's. Instead, the irreversibility of time and the origins of information are properties of the universe that hinge on additional physical laws governing the behavior of large collections of particles. This is a wild theoretical territory, where the basic idea of a trajectory—the path along which something travels—loses its meaning. Surprisingly, when trajectories become meaningless is when time emerges.

The irreversibility of time and the ubiquity of information combine to create an even bigger puzzle. As we will see, the irreversibility of time is connected to a universal march from order to disorder. Yet for as long as we have been aware, our planet has been doing the opposite. The quantity of information in our planet appears to be steadily growing, not shrinking.

The ubiquitous growth of information on our planet was a fact that flew in the face of nineteenth-century physics. Although nineteenth-century physicists could see the complexity of the world accelerating as they looked out their windows, they understood Boltzmann's discovery that information is mostly destroyed as time goes by. The sound created by a guitar disappears as the sound waves penetrate the air. The ripples created by a pebble thrown into a pond disappear as the pond goes back to its resting state. This loss of information was explained by the physics discovered in the nineteenth century, but the growth of information that continues to take place in well-defined pockets of the universe was not.

The attention devoted to this paradox of order grew during the nineteenth century when Charles Lyell and Charles Darwin emphasized that our planet was not six thousand years old, as the Bible had suggested, but billions of years old. This impressive new fact implied that the anomalous increase of information that everyone observed had been going on for billions of years. But anomalies are short-lived—they should not be eternal. So the only conclusion that could be drawn from this obvious contradiction was that something was missing from our understanding of nature. Order was growing, but nobody knew why.

Boltzmann's foremost success came in an 1878 paper showing that systems composed of many particles tended toward states that had as little information as possible. This is what is known as the second law of thermodynamics, which had been anticipated a few decades earlier by Rudolf Clausius, albeit in a more cumbersome formulation. The second law of thermodynamics states that the entropy of closed physical systems always tends to increase, meaning that systems march from order to disorder. Think of dropping a dash of ink into a glass of clear water. The initial state, the one in which the drop of ink is localized in a gorgeous swirl, is information-rich. There are few ways for the ink to be localized, but many ways in which it could be distributed more or less uniformly in the glass. The final state, in which the ink has diffused, is information-poor because there are many states that are equivalent to that. So when you drop a bit of ink in a glass of water you see the arrow of time moving. It moves from an information-rich state to an information-poor state. As time goes by, the universe moves from rare configurations to common ones, and Boltzmann's theory explained that perfectly.

Yet the universe is filled with examples that are not like the drop of ink, examples where information and complexity are seen to increase, such as the development of human babies or the natural reforestation of a burned-over forest. So where does that information come from? The universes predicted by Boltzmann and Maxwell, and later refined by the thermodynamics of Helmholtz, Gibbs, and Einstein, were universes that evolved into homogeneous soups—soups in which there was no information and energy was no longer free (that is, there was no energy available to perform work).[3]

During the twentieth century our understanding of the arrow of time and the physical origins of information became reconciled with the physical nature of reality. New theories were able to show that information was not an anomaly but something to be expected. These theories did not contradict the dynamics of Einstein and Newton or the statistical mechanics of Boltzmann, since they showed that the origins of information and the arrow of time hinged on additional physical principles and considerations. The key thinker in this area was the Russian-born and Belgian-raised statistical physicist Ilya Prigogine. Prigogine was awarded the 1977 Nobel Prize in Chemistry "for his contributions to non-equilibrium thermodynamics, particularly the theory of dissipative structures."[4] Prigogine produced many important insights, but the one that is of concern to us here is the idea that *information emerges naturally in the steady states of physical systems that are out of equilibrium.* That statement, which summarizes the physical origins of information, sounds awfully complicated. Yet if we go carefully through a sequence of examples, we will realize that it is not. So in the next paragraphs I will unpack the meaning of Prigogine's statement to a point at which its meaning will become obvious.

To understand the physical origins of information we need to understand a few things first. One is the idea of a steady state. The second is the difference between a dynamic steady state and a static steady state. A very simple case of a static steady state is a marble dropped into a bowl. We all know what happens here. After a short period of time the marble sits quietly at the bottom of the bowl. This represents a static steady state.

A more interesting case is that of a box filled with gas. If we put gas inside a box and wait for a bit, the amount of gas in the right side of the box will be equal to the amount in the left side of the box. The steady state of a box filled with gas, however, is not analogous to that of a marble sitting in the bottom of a bowl. In a box filled with gas, the molecules are not all resting in a fixed position. They are moving constantly, and the steady state is reached when the number of gas molecules traveling from left to right is equal to the number of molecules traveling from right to left. The box with gas (like the example of a drop of ink fully diffused within a glass of water) represents a case of a dynamic steady state.

Now let's consider the steady state of a non-equilibrium system. The classic example in this case is the whirlpool that forms when you empty a bathtub. As soon as you remove the stopper and water starts racing down the drain, the water above the drain begins to organize into a whirlpool. The whirlpool is a steady state, since it is stable as long as there is water flowing in the system. It is also an information-rich state, since whirlpools are rare configurations of water molecules that do not appear spontaneously in still water.[5] Unlike still water, whirlpools are organized structures in which the water molecules are not going in random directions, but have a speed and trajectory that is correlated with that of the water molecules traveling next to them. The information-rich state of a whirlpool emerges naturally—it is something that we get for free in an out-of-equilibrium system. Going back to our original sentence, we can say that the whirlpool is an example of information that emerges naturally in the steady state of a physical system that is out of equilibrium.

Yet the whirlpool is not our only example. There are many other examples of order that emerges spontaneously in out-of-equilibrium systems, such as swirls of cigarette smoke, the hypnotic movement of a campfire, and even the glow of your computer screen since your computer screen is definitely out of equilibrium when it is turned on. You and your mobile phone are also examples of physical systems that are out of equilibrium. In your case, you eat to stay out of equilibrium, while in the case of your cellphone you recharge it every night.

Prigogine realized that although Boltzmann's theory was correct, it did not apply to what we observe on Earth because our planet is an out-of-equilibrium pocket inside a larger system—the universe—that is moving toward equilibrium. In fact, our planet has never been close to any form of equilibrium. The energy of the sun and the nuclear decay taking place in the Earth's core drive our planet out of equilibrium, providing the energy required for information to emerge. We can think of our planet as a little whirlpool of information in an otherwise vast and barren cosmos.

Prigogine realized that to understand the information-rich nature of the universe, he needed to understand the statistical properties of systems that were out of equilibrium. These statistical properties are different from the properties of the systems Boltzmann studied, and they include the cases where information emerges naturally. Prigogine's breakthrough included the derivation of some of the mathematical laws and principles that govern the behavior of out-of-equilibrium systems. His work showed that the universe is organized in a peculiar manner, with *information being hidden on the other side of chaos.* Consider boiling water in a pan. First, imagine turning the heat on just a little bit. If you do that, a small quantity of water at the bottom of the pan will warm up. These molecules will start moving around a bit faster, but if you turn off the heat quickly, the water in the pan will never self-organize into an information-rich state. Now imagine leaving the heat on longer. As the water molecules start moving more, the fluid becomes turbulent. It is chaotic. This is a state that already contains information, much like that of the swirls of cigarette smoke. Now keep the heat on long enough for the pan to enter a dynamic steady state of convection. Here, organized flow will emerge. So after chaos, the system organizes into a state that is highly organized, full of correlations and information. Prigogine showed that the steady states that matter reaches in systems that are out of equilibrium tend to be organized. After chaos there is information.

The fact that out-of-equilibrium systems are characterized by information-rich steady states helps us understand where information comes from. In an out-of-equilibrium system, such as Earth, the emergence of information is expected. It is no longer an anomaly. The bad news, however, is that entropy is always lurking on the borders of information-rich anomalies, waiting to devour these anomalies as soon as it gets the chance. Bathtub whirlpools vanish as soon as we put the stopper back in the drain or run out of water. This might lead us to think that the universe is quick at taking away the information-rich steady states that out-of-equilibrium systems give us for free. Yet information has found ways to fight back. As a result, we live on a planet where information is "sticky" enough to be recombined and created. This stickiness, which is essential for the emergence of life and economies, also hinges on additional fundamental physical properties.

The first mechanism that contributes to the stickiness of information involves the idea of thermodynamic potentials. Once again this sounds complicated, but it is not. What we need to know here is that the steady states of physical systems can be described as minimums of mathematical functions, which are known as thermodynamic potentials. We are all familiar with the basic idea of potentials from high school physics, since we know that marbles end up at the bottom of bowls because in that state there is a minimum of potential energy. Now, the thing is that not all of the steady states of physical systems minimize energy. Many steady states minimize or maximize other quantities (for example, a gas sitting quietly in a box maximizes entropy). Yet we do not need to describe all of these quantities here, since we are interested primarily in the potentials that rule out-of-equilibrium systems. So what is the potential that out-of-equilibrium systems such as our bathtub whirlpool minimize? In 1947 Prigogine showed that *the steady state of out-of-equilibrium systems minimizes the production of entropy.*[6] What this means is that out-of-equilibrium systems self-organize into steady states in which order emerges spontaneously, minimizing the destruction of information.

Prigogine derived his principle by considering a system close to equilibrium. This was a system characterized by one steady state and multiple transient states. This is a fairly narrow case, and his principle therefore could not be immediately applied to systems that were far from equilibrium, which are systems that can "choose" among multiple steady states. In fact, even though it is still a matter of debate, some people have postulated that far-from-equilibrium systems choose the steady state that maximizes entropy production.[7] This principle of maximum entropy production does not contradict Prigogine's principle of minimum entropy production, however, because the steady state of maximum entropy production still produces less entropy than transient states. Still, we need to be careful not to get carried away by this conversation, since our goal is not to go into the complexities of non-equilibrium statistical physics but to explain the origins of information. So I will leave the question of the potential that rules far-from-equilibrium systems open and conclude that this potential, whether it is the minimization of entropy production, the maximization of entropy production, or the degree of irreversibility of the statistical process, is nevertheless characterized by self-organizing states that are rich in correlations, are less dissipative than transient states, and produce the physical order that is a prerequisite for life. As Prigogine and Grégoire Nicolis note in a brilliant 1971 paper discussing the connection between non-equilibrium systems and life: "Generally speaking, the destruction of structures is the situation which prevails in the neighbourhood of thermodynamic equilibrium. On the contrary, . . . creation of structures may occur, with specific non-linear kinetic laws beyond the domain of stability of the states showing the usual thermodynamic behaviour."[8]

Statistical-physics systems generate information and hold on to it when they are out of equilibrium, but their fluidity makes it hard to see how these systems can hold on to information for too long. Whirlpools disappear suddenly, and the smoke of cigarettes loses its bohemian beauty as it diffuses into hazy clouds. The statistical properties of non-equilibrium systems can help us understand the nonhuman origins of information but not its endurance. Yet it is the endurance of information that allows information to be recombined and allows life and the economy to emerge. The endurance of information is therefore as important as its origin, since without it the recombinations we need for information to beget more information cannot take place. Yet the endurance of information is not guaranteed in the laws that explain its origin. Once again, there must be something else going on.

As Erwin Schrödinger, the 1933 Nobel laureate in physics, noted in his 1944 book *What Is Life?*, we cannot understand the permanence of physically embodied information by thinking only about the fluid systems that we have used in our examples. Cigarette smoke, whirlpools, drops of ink, and gases are all fluids, and much of their evanescence comes from this fluidity. So the second reason information is sticky and can be recombined is because it is embodied in solids. Once again, consider the bathtub whirlpool, but now assume you have a magic wand that allows you to freeze or crystallize the bathtub and the whirlpool with a single twist of your wrist.[9] Take an imaginary icepick and chisel the whirlpool out of its icy confines. What you hold in your hand is a little quantum of information. As long as you don't unfreeze the whirlpool, some of the information that was present in that information-rich steady state will remain there.[10] By solidifying the whirlpool, we trapped information that was generated in a fluid world and gained a crystal of information that we can use to help construct the complexity of our world.

To the best of my knowledge, freezing whirlpools is not physically possible, but it gives us a good mental picture that we can use to understand the importance of solids in the permanence and evolution of information. In *What Is Life?* Schrödinger strongly emphasized that solids were essential to explain the information-rich nature of life. Schrödinger—as well as every biologist in the world at the time—understood that the information required to build a biological organism was hidden somewhere inside the cell, in either proteins or DNA.[11] From a physical perspective, both proteins and DNA are technically crystals; more precisely, they are aperiodic crystals (structures that do not repeat each other but contain long-range correlations). Think of a sheet of music where the same four notes repeat over and over. The information carried by that sheet would be minimal compared to one in which variations and departures are prevalent. Schrödinger understood that aperiodicity was needed to store information, since a regular crystal would be unable to carry much information: "The gene is most certainly not just a homogeneous drop of liquid. It is probably a large protein molecule, in which every atom, every radical, every heterocyclic ring plays an individual role, more or less different from that played by any of the other similar atoms, radicals, or rings." According to Schrödinger, the phenomenon of life hinged on both the aperiodicity of biological molecules and their solid, crystalline nature. The aperiodicity was essential for the molecule to embody information, and the solid nature of the molecule was essential for this information to last.

So by combining the ideas of Prigogine and Schrödinger, we can understand where information comes from (the steady state of non-equilibrium systems) and why it sticks around (because it is stored in solids). The poetic oddity of this combination is that it tells us that our universe is both frozen and dynamic. From a physical perspective, a solid is "frozen" because its structure is stable to the thermal fluctuations of the environment.[12] Our cities are made of solids, such as cars, buildings, bus stops, subways, and sidewalks. Our homes are made of solids, such as kitchen sinks, refrigerators, dishes, lightbulbs, and washing machines. Our cells are also made of solids, which are the tens of thousands of proteins that run the cellular show. Yet cars and proteins are solids that can move around. Cities and cells are dynamic systems where solids move with respect to one another. The solid nature of these objects allows us to accumulate information at a low cost, since solids shield the information stored in them from the bloody claws of entropy, even if it's for just a short cosmic time.

But there is more to the growth of information than crystalline solids and dynamic whirlpools. For information to truly grow, the universe needs one more trick. This is the ability of matter to process information, or the ability of matter to compute.

Consider a tree. A tree, in its semi-"frozen" state, is a computer powered by sunlight. A tree in New England reacts to the length of the day, running a different program in the summer than in the winter. It figures out when to shed its leaves and when to sprout new ones. A tree processes the information that is available in its environment. Its proteins, organized in signaling pathways, help the tree figure out how to grow its roots toward the water it needs, how to activate an immune response when it is threatened by pathogens, and how to push its leaves toward the sun it craves. A tree does not have the consciousness or language that we have, but it shares with us a general ability to process information. A tree has knowhow, even though the way in which it processes information is unlike our mental abilities and more similar to the processes our own bodies do without knowing how: digestion, immunity, hormonal regulation, and so on.

While a tree is technically a computer, its power source is not an electrical outlet but the sun. A tree is a computer that, just like us, cannot run MATLAB, but unlike computers and us, it has the knowhow to run photosynthesis. Trees process information, and they are able to do so because they are steady states of out-of-equilibrium systems. Trees embody knowhow, which they use to survive.

But since a tree is alive I cannot use it to argue that computation precedes life (although it is a convincing example of computation predating humans). To illustrate the prebiotic nature of the ability of matter to process information, we need to consider a more fundamental system. Here is where the chemical systems that fascinated Prigogine come in handy.

Consider a set of chemical reactions that takes a set of compounds {I} and transforms them into a set of outputs {O} via a set of intermediate compounds {M}. Now consider feeding this system with a steady flow of {I}. If the flow of {I} is small, then the system will settle into a steady state where the intermediate inputs {M} will be produced and consumed in such a way that their numbers do not fluctuate much. The system will reach a state of equilibrium. In most chemical systems, however, once we crank up the flow of {I} this equilibrium will become unstable, meaning that the steady state of the system will be replaced by two or more stable steady states that are different from the original state of equilibrium.[13] When these new steady states emerge, the system will need to "choose" among them, meaning that it will have to move to one or the other, breaking the symmetry of the system and developing a history that is marked by those choices. If we crank up the inflow of the input compounds {I} even further, these new steady states will become unstable and additional new steady states will emerge. This multiplication of steady states can lead these chemical reactions to highly organized states, such as those exhibited by molecular clocks, which are chemical oscillators, compounds that change periodically from one type to another. But does such a simple chemical system have the ability to process information?

Now consider that we can push the system to one of these steady states by changing the concentration of inputs {I}. Such a system will be "computing," since it will be generating outputs that are conditional on the inputs it is ingesting. It would be a chemical transistor. In an awfully crude way this chemical system models a primitive metabolism. In an even cruder way, it is a model of a cell differentiating from one cell type to another—the cell types can be viewed abstractly as the dynamic steady states of these systems, as the complex systems biologist Stuart Kauffman suggested decades ago.[14]

Highly interacting out-of-equilibrium systems, whether they are trees reacting to the change of seasons or chemical systems processing information about the inputs they receive, teach us that matter can compute. These systems tell us that computation precedes the origins of life just as much as information does. The chemical changes encoded by these systems are modifying the information encoded in these chemical compounds, and therefore they represent a fundamental form of computation. Life is a consequence of the ability of matter to compute.

Finally, we need to explain how all of this relates to the irreversibility of time. After all, this is where the chapter started. To explain this, I will use once again the work of Prigogine, and as an example, I will invite you to imagine a large box filled with trillions of ping-pong balls.[15]

Imagine that the ping-pong balls collide with one another without losing energy, so these interactions never cease. Next, assume that you started observing the system when all of the ping-pong balls were located neatly in one quadrant of the box, but also were endowed with enough kinetic energy—or speed—to eventually scatter all around the box. This is similar to the drop-of-ink example we used before.

In this simple statistical system, the question of the reversibility of time is the question of whether it is possible, at any given point in time, to reverse the motion of the ping-pong balls such that time is seen to run backward. That is, is it possible to put the ping-pong balls on a trajectory where the final state is the neat arrangement that we defined as the initial configuration?

Thinking of what happens when we run this "movie" forward is easy. Ping-pong balls fill up the box with their incessant motion, ending up in what we now know as a dynamic steady state. But let's give the time-reversal experiment a shot. To make things easy I will assume that we have two machines. One of the machines is able to take any number of balls and modify their velocities instantly if we provide the machine with an input file containing the desired velocities for each ball. This machine has infinite precision, but it executes instructions only with the precision of the information that it is fed. That is, if positions and velocities are provided with a precision of two digits (i.e., speed in centimeters per second), then the machine will assign the velocities of the balls with only that precision, making all unspecified decimals (i.e., millimeters per second and beyond) random. The second machine we have available measures the position and velocity of each ball with a finite but arbitrarily large precision. So the question is, can we use these two imaginary machines to reverse the velocities of the system such that the "movie" plays backward?

Let's first try the experiment by reversing the velocities of each ball with a very coarse precision. For instance, if the velocity of a given ball in the x direction is $v_x = 0.2342562356237128 \ldots$ [mts/sec], we simply reverse it by taking the first two digits (i.e., we make the new $v_x = -0.23$). Will this simple reversal be enough to make the movie play backward? The answer is certainly not. A system of trillions of ping-pong balls that never lose energy, like the one I am describing here, is by definition chaotic, meaning that small differences in initial conditions grow exponentially over time. The chaotic nature of the system implies that a precision of two digits is not enough to put the balls on a trajectory that will naturally evolve back to its original configuration. But is this just a matter of precision, or is there a fundamental constraint at play? Given enough precision in our measurements and actions, can we reverse time?

Armed with our imaginary machines, we can rerun this thought experiment with greater precision, but as long as that precision is finite, we will not be able to reverse time. Instead of using a couple of digits, we could specify velocity with ten, twenty, or a hundred digits. But the reversal of time will still not be achieved because in a chaotic system, the imprecisions of our measurements will grow to dominate the system. In mathematical language, we can say that this is a case where the importance of digits is inverted. Normally when we have a number with many digits, the digits to the left are more important than those to the right (especially in your bank account). But in a chaotic system this is not the case, since in such a system it is the last digit of the measurement, not the first one, that grows to become dominant. Yet no matter how precise our measurement, there is always a digit to the right of any number. So even without bringing in Heisenberg's uncertainty principle (which will limit our precision to a few tens of digits), we can conclude that the movie will always look as if it is playing forward, except for the brief period of time in which we are injecting energy into the system by changing the velocities of the particles with our machines.

So time is irreversible in a statistical system because the chaotic nature of systems of many particles implies that an infinite amount of information would be needed to reverse the evolution of the system. This also means that statistical systems cannot go backward because there are an infinite number of paths that are compatible with any present. As statistical systems move forward, they quickly forget how to go back. This infiniteness is what Prigogine calls the *entropy barrier,* and it is what provides a perspective of time that is not spatialized like the theories of time advanced by Newton and Einstein. For Prigogine, the past is not just unreachable; it simply does not exist. There *is* no past, although there *was* a past. In our universe, **there is no past, and no future, but only a present that is being calculated at every instant**. This instantaneous nature of reality is deep because it helps us connect statistical physics with computation. The instantaneous universe of Prigogine implies that the past is unreachable because it is incomputable at the micro level. Prigogine's entropy barrier forbids the present to evolve into the past, except in idealized systems, like a pendulum or planetary orbits, which look the same going forward and backward (when there is no dissipation involved).

*　　*　　*

We started this chapter by asking ourselves about the irreversibility of time and the origins of information. We learned that when put together, these questions pose a puzzle, since time moves from order to disorder even though the complexity of our world is seen to increase. The universal increase of entropy appears to contradict the growth of information, but in fact it does not, since the universe has some tricks up its sleeve that allow information to emerge in well-defined pockets. These are pockets where free energy is abundant, but also where the range of temperatures is mild enough for solids to exist, as information lasts longer when preserved in solids.

The thermodynamics of the universe I described in this chapter help us understand the circumstances under which information is allowed to emerge. Yet the ability of the universe to beget the complexity we see out our windows is not an immediate consequence of these simple mechanisms. For information to truly grow, the universe needed one more trick. This is the ability of matter to compute.

This computational ability of matter, which can be embodied both in simple chemical systems and in complex life-forms such as trees or us, is the key capacity that allows information to grow explosively in the pocket of the universe we call home. This computational capacity, and its relationship to humans and the networks that humans form, will be the focus of the third part of the book, which explores the ability of systems to accumulate knowledge and knowhow. We will need this computational capacity, and the constraints defined by its human embodiment, to explain the growth of information in society.

But before we go there, we need to first understand the physicality of the information that relates more closely to humans—the information that we produce with our human knowledge and knowhow. This is not the physicality of DNA or of frozen whirlpools, but the physicality of the simple and complex products we produce and exchange, from a macaroni necklace to a jumbo skyliner. So where we are headed next is into a thorough description of the objects that make our economy, focusing on the information that products embody and the implicit abilities that this information helps them carry. This will allow us to see products not just as physical embodiments of information but also as the vehicles we use to communicate something more important than messages: the practical uses of knowledge and knowhow.

PART II

Crystallized Imagination

This world is but a canvas to our imagination.
—Henry David Thoreau

I'm often tired of processing information. I move around as fast as I can, but the world is overwhelmingly vast and fast. I answer emails, pick up things, comment on drafts, prepare slides, give talks, think of agreements, think of arguments, think of website designs, referee papers, write proposals, prepare figures, think of algorithms, take pictures, board planes, pack luggage, give advice, receive advice, make sandwiches, press buttons on the elevator, try to remember things, and of course suffer at the keyboard while rearranging words.

I am a small mobile neuron in a vast social and economic universe. I move around, often not knowing where I am going. Pulled around by signals, I struggle to adapt as I attempt to balance my desires to make something with my desires to live a social life. Of course, that's not always easy.

And that, in a nutshell, is what life is all about: moving around and processing information, helping information grow while interacting in a social context. We spend our lives passing on meaningless objects and meaningful messages: objects that augment our capacity to process information, and messages that affect our behaviors and attitudes toward others. We form social structures to compensate for our limited capacities, and these social structures learn how to process information. And thus we beget information in objects and words. We create our surroundings, from the most meaningful to the meaningless, as we inadvertently slave away to serve the growth of information.

In the next pages I will describe the social and economic mechanisms that contribute to the growth of information in the economy. These mechanisms are extensions of the three principles I just described for physical systems, but here they have been recast to incorporate the complexities of social and economic systems.*

Our society's ability to accumulate information requires flows of energy, the physical storage of information in solid objects, and of course our collective ability to compute. The flow of energy that keeps our planet's information growing is clearly that coming from the sun. Plants capture that energy and transform it into sugar, and over long periods of time they degrade into the mineral fuel we know as oil. But as a species, we have also developed an amazing capacity to make information last. We have learned to accumulate information in objects, starting from the time we built our first stone axes to the invention of the latest computer.

---

* Though often not in the traditional language of economics.

The creation of these solid objects requires flows of energy, but also our distributed capacity to compute. Our species' capacity to compute requires social networks to function, and it is therefore affected by institutions and technologies. These institutions and technologies involve the fragmentation of human languages, discrimination, trust, and communication and transportation technologies, among others. Inadequate institutions and technologies can trample our ability to form the networks we need to accumulate knowledge and knowhow, limiting the rate at which we can make information grow.

This part of the book will be dedicated to the solid objects that humans create to accumulate information. For poetic and technical reasons I will call these objects *crystals of imagination*. Part III will be dedicated to exploring the idea of society as a computer and will focus on the mechanisms that limit the formation of the social networks we need to accumulate knowledge and knowhow. Part IV will bring in data, focusing on empirical connections that we can use to validate the predictions of these theories and bring this idea together with traditional literature describing the process of economic growth and development.

46

Man processing information in the form of shoes. Riyadh, Saudi Arabia.

People exchanging conversations and packets of information. St. Petersburg, Russia.

An information processor in a resting state. Cartagena, Colombia.

A family sharing messages while consuming energy. Santiago, Chile.

A cathedral of long- and short-term correlations. St. Petersburg, Russia.

Discarded information. Somerville, Massachusetts.

4

Out of Our Heads!

We talk much of imagination. We talk of the imagi-
nation of poets, the imagination of artists, and I am
inclined to think that in general we don't know very
much exactly what we are talking about.

It is [that] which penetrates into the unseen
worlds around us, the worlds of science. It is that
which feels and discovers what is, the real which
we see not, which exists not for our senses.

—ADA LOVELACE

That's all the motorcycle is, a system of concepts
worked out in steel. There's no part in it, no shape in
it, that is not out of someone's mind.

—ROBERT M. PIRSIG

Consider two types of apples: those that grow on trees and you buy
at the supermarket, and those that are designed in Silicon Valley.
Both are traded in the economy, and both embody information,
whether in biological cells or silicon chips. The main difference
between them is not their number of parts or their ability to perform functions—edible apples are the result of tens of thousands
of genes that perform sophisticated biochemical functions. The

main difference between apples and Apples is that the apples we eat existed first in the world and then in our heads, while the Apples we use to check our email existed first in someone's head and then in the world. Both of these apples are products and embody information, but only one of them—the silicon Apple—is a crystal of imagination.[1]

Thinking about products as crystals of imagination tells us that products do not just embody information but also imagination. This is information that we have generated through mental computations and then disembodied by creating an object that mimics the one we had in our head. Edible apples existed before we had a name for them, a price for them, or a market for them. They were present in the world. As a concept, apples were simply imported into our minds. On the other hand, iPhones and iPads are mental exports rather than imports, since they are products that were begotten in our minds before they became part of our world. So the main difference between apples and Apples resides in the source of their physical order rather than in their embodiment of physical order. Both products are packets of information, but only one of them is a crystal of imagination. In this chapter I will emphasize the imaginary origin of the information embodied in products, as this is a fundamental characteristic of the type of information that humans grow and accumulate.

To grasp the concept of crystallized imagination, consider the personal narratives of two of my Media Lab colleagues Hugh Herr and Ed Boyden. Hugh is a passionate mountain climber who knows the risks of the sport well. At a young age he lost both of his legs to frostbite on Mount Washington. In his late forties, however, Hugh walks proudly across the MIT campus. He is a man of few words; I guess he does not need them after having built his own legs.

Hugh's case is particularly inspiring. He was born in a world where the possibility of buying robotic limbs did not exist. Upon his exit, our species will have the capacity to recover limbs through robotic extensions that connect to our nervous system, and maybe even restore the feeling of touch.

Hugh belongs to a research field involving a large number of people, but he is also the perfect example of someone we can associate with the creation of a new packet of physically embodied information. Through the creation of objects, Hugh and his colleagues are endowing our species with a new set of capacities, expanding what is humanly possible.[2] The most poetic part of Hugh's accomplishment, however, is not that he is walking on robotic legs but that he is walking on solidified pieces of his own imagination.

Ed's case is different from Hugh's but also tremendously inspiring. Over the past decade Ed has helped develop the field of optogenetics, a method to stimulate neurons using light. Together with other researchers, Ed is helping invent future interfaces between humans and machines. Over the long run Ed and his colleagues will give rise to what I call colloquially "a USB port for the brain."

A USB port for the brain is a great example of a technology that will open a universe of future possibilities. These range from the recovery of biological functions in ways that expand Hugh's vision to the future of gaming and the Internet. The future will change with this technology in ways that we are poorly positioned to imagine or judge. Yet there is a simple aspect that both Hugh's and Ed's work have in common: both are creating objects that crystallize imagination, and by doing so, they are endowing our species with new capacities.

Thinking about Hugh's and Ed's work in terms of crystallized imagination probably seems poetically justified, but it may not be so obvious that it is a useful way to think about products more generally. As we will see, thinking about products as crystals of imagination will help us understand people's desire for products, but it will also allow us to reinterpret important economic processes. As an example of the latter, consider international trade.

Thinking of product exports in terms of crystallized imagination tells us that we live in a world in which some countries are net importers of imagination, while others are net exporters of it. The idea of crystallized imagination tells us that a country's export structure carries information about more than just its abundance of capital and labor. A country's export structure is a fingerprint that tells us about the ability of people in that country to create tangible instantiations of imaginary objects, such as automobiles, espresso machines, subway cars, and motorcycles, and of course about the myriad of specific factors that are needed to create these sophisticated products. In fact, the composition of a country's exports informs us about the knowledge and knowhow that are embodied in that country's population.[3]

Since exports and imports encompass the exchange of embodied imagination, it is natural to ask when the balance of trade between a pair of countries—monetary value of exports minus imports—runs opposite to that pair's balance of imagination. Finding these examples using international trade data is relatively easy, especially when we are empowered with a visualization engine such as the Observatory of Economic Complexity, which Alex Simoes created as his master's thesis in my research group at the MIT Media Lab (http://atlas.media.mit.edu).

One example of a balance of trade that runs opposite to the balance of imagination is that of Chile and Korea (see Figures 1 and 2). In 2012, Chile exported $4.6 billion worth of products to Korea, mostly refined and unrefined copper.[4] That same year, the exports from Korea to Chile were worth only about $2.5 billion, mostly vehicles and vehicle parts.[5] Chile clearly had a positive trade balance with Korea in 2012. Chile's imagination balance with Korea, however, was clearly negative, since Chile did not embody much imagination in the goods it exported, but it imported plenty of embodied imagination in the goods it bought.

Figure 1. Products that Chile exported to South Korea in 2012. Total exports USD 4.61B

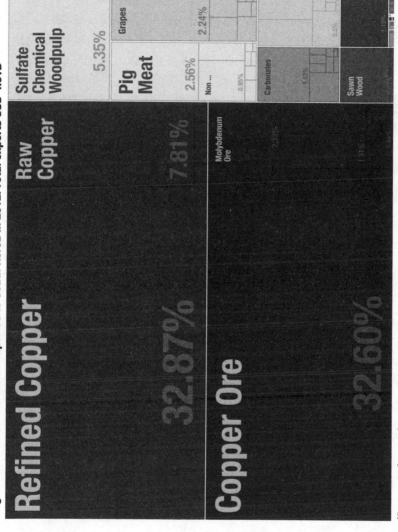

(Source: atlas.media.mit.edu)

Figure 2. Products that South Korea exported to Chile in 2012. Total exports USD 2.54B

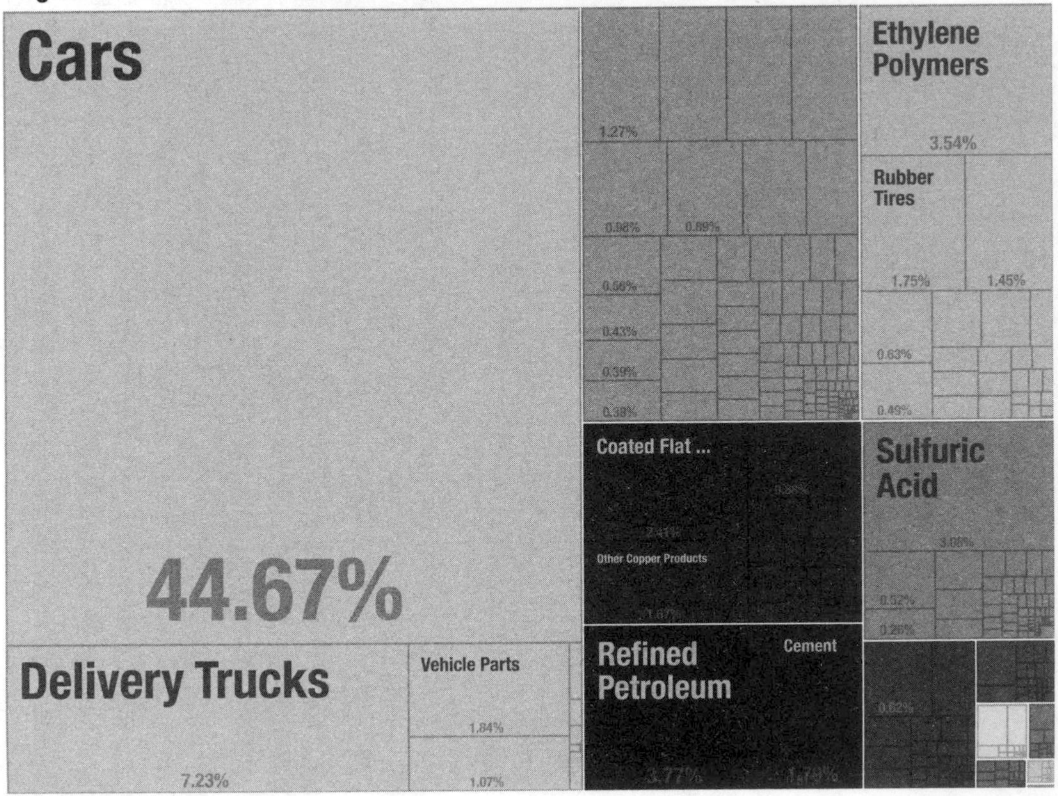
Cars
44.67%
Delivery Trucks
7.23%
Vehicle Parts
1.84%
1.07%
1.27%
0.98%
0.89%
0.56%
0.43%
0.39%
0.38%
Ethylene Polymers
3.54%
Rubber Tires
1.75%
1.45%
0.63%
0.49%
Coated Flat ...
Other Copper Products
Sulfuric Acid
0.52%
0.26%
Refined Petroleum
Cement
3.77%
1.79%
0.62%

(Source: atlas.media.mit.edu)

Another example is Brazil and China. In 2012 Brazil exported products worth more than $41 billion to China, and it imported products worth only $33.4 billion (see Figures 3 and 4). Brazil has enjoyed a positive trade balance with China during recent years but a negative imagination balance, since its trade with the largest Asian economy involves mostly the exchange of iron ore and soybeans for electronics, chemicals, and even processed metals.

So classic economic concepts, such as the balance of trade between two countries, seem incomplete once we reinterpret products as crystals of imagination. When we start seeing products as embodiments of human imagination, we realize that there is an alternative to the balance of trade. This is the balance of imagination, which involves the exchange of imagination that piggybacks the concoctions of atoms we buy and sell.

Understanding the world in terms of exchanges of embodied imagination can also help us challenge prevalent narratives. A narrative that is prevalent in many developing countries, and which is often used in politicized environments, equates the exports of raw materials with an act of exploitation. Here *exploitation* refers not to the exploitative dynamics that can emerge within an industry but to a more general idea that focuses on the origins of the economic value of what is being extracted. As I will show in the next pages, that economic value comes not from those involved in extractive activities but from the imagination of others who are usually detached from the extractive processes.

I am quite familiar with the general exploitation narrative, having spent the first twenty-four years of my life in the long strip of coast and mountains known as Chile. Chile has a long mining tradition or as I like to say, Chile is heavily involved in "atomic ranching." But this was not always the case. During the nineteenth century Chile's wealth came mostly from the export of saltpeter, a mineral used as a fertilizer and as an ingredient in gunpowder. Saltpeter made the Chilean economy boom. At the turn of the

Figure 3. Products that Brazil exported to China in 2012. Total exports USD 41.3B

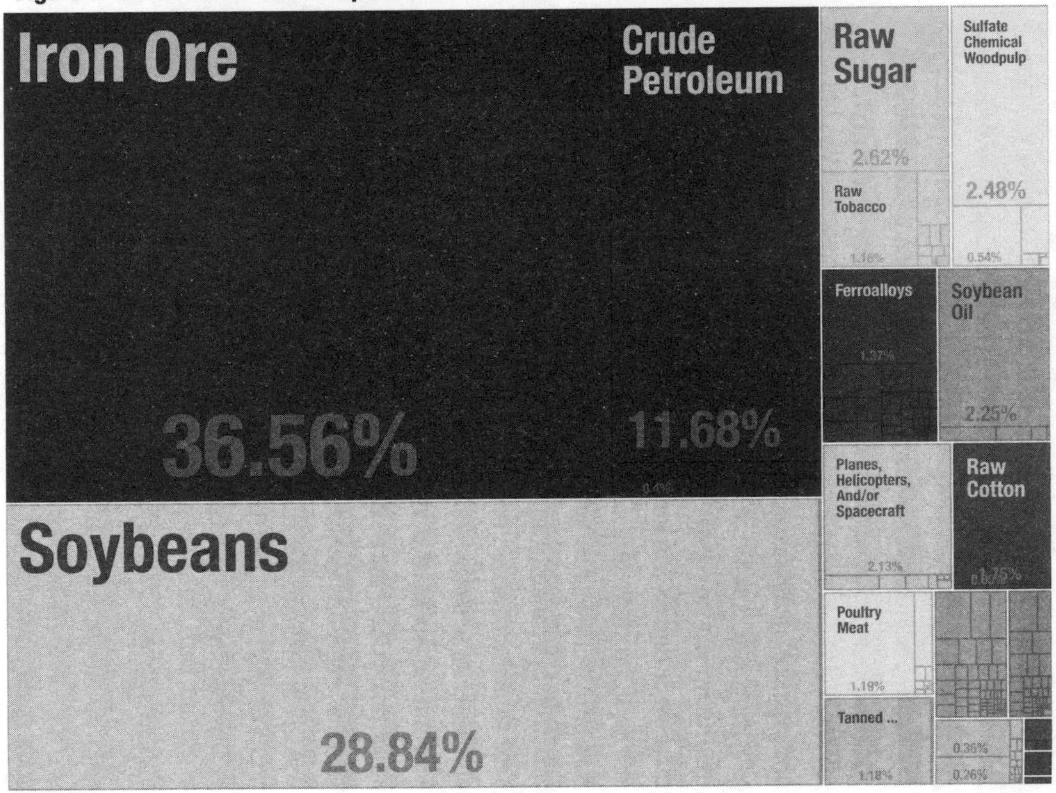

(Source: atlas.media.mit.edu)

Figure 4. Products that China exported to Brazil in 2012. Total exports USD 33.4B

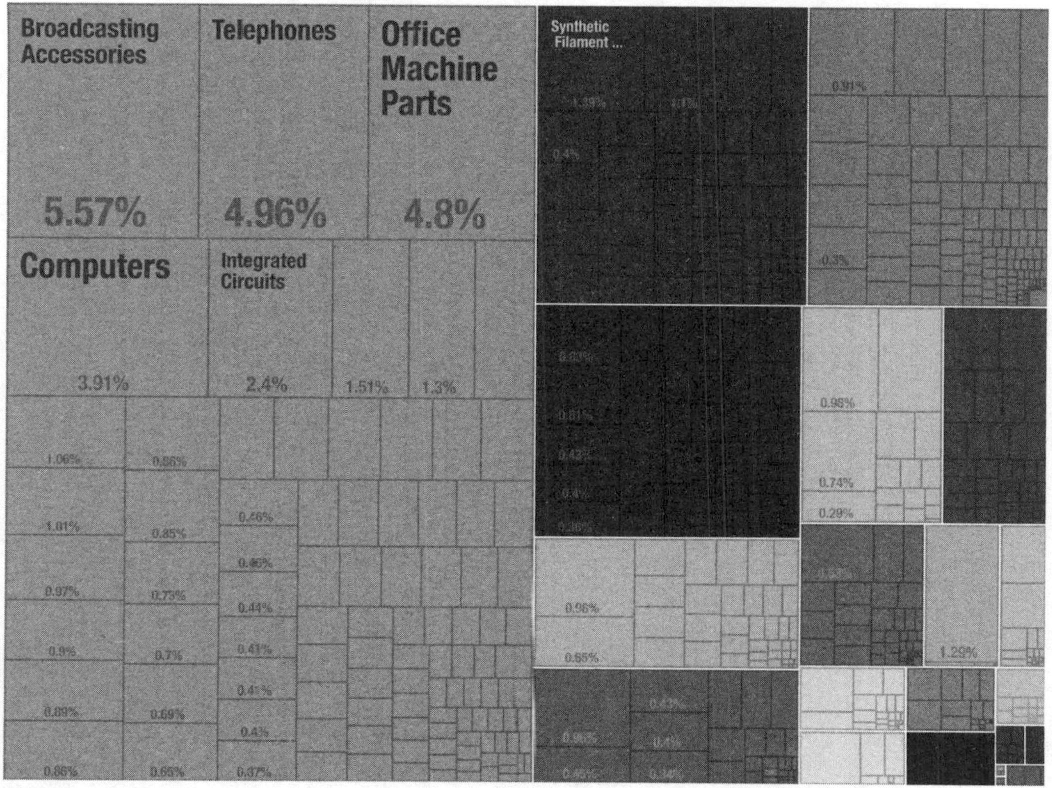

(Source: atlas.media.mit.edu)

twentieth century Chile had an income per capita that was larger than that of Spain, Sweden, or Finland.[6] Things were good, but the pendulum was about to swing the other way.

In 1909 the German chemists Fritz Haber and Carl Bosch discovered an inexpensive way of synthesizing saltpeter on an industrial scale. Their ability to glue atoms together threw a wrench into the gears of the Chilean economy. On top of that, the opening of the Panama Canal in 1914 marginalized the need for ships to travel along the Chilean coastline, dealing the country's economy a second grave blow. Between 1910 and 1921 the Chilean economy shrank at an annualized rate of 2 percent.

At the turn of the twenty-first century Chile continued to be an export-oriented economy, but one focused on the export of copper rather than saltpeter.[7] Chile's case is not bizarre; in fact, it is quite common. Copper is to Chile what natural gas is to Bolivia, tea and flowers are to Kenya, radioactive minerals are to Namibia, soybeans are to Argentina, diamonds are to Sierra Leone and Botswana, and oil is to Nigeria, Saudi Arabia, Angola, Congo, Kazakhstan, Algeria, Equatorial Guinea, Russia, Venezuela, and many others.

The availability of copper in the Chilean Andes is vast, and Chile's ability to hold copper atoms hostage contributes importantly to Chileans' ability to import crystals of imagination. In 2012 the value of Chilean copper exports surpassed $40 billion. That is roughly $2,300 for every man, woman, and child in Chile, or $6,900 per family, since the average Chilean family is composed of three people.[8]

But why is copper so valuable? Why is the rest of the world willing to pay Chile billions of dollars every year for what are literally rocks?

Copper is a good conductor. It is not as good a conductor as gold, but it is certainly more abundant and less expensive. Copper is used in most of the crystals of imagination that make use of our knowledge of electricity, including the systems we use to generate and transmit power and the electrical systems of cars.

But like all minerals, copper does not come with a book of recipes that can help those who are endowed with copper to anticipate its potential uses. Early on people used copper to create primitive forms of armor (for which copper, heavy and malleable, is not ideal), tools, and kitchenware. But these items did not produce a demand for copper that would justify the massive excavations that are used to extract copper today. In the nineteenth century our demand for copper began to change, as our understanding of electricity begot a plethora of products that increased the global demand for copper and required new efforts to dig up these green rocks.

A major breakthrough was Faraday's law of induction, which taught us how to generate electricity by jiggling a magnet in front of a coil. Other champions of the electric revolution included Nicola Tesla, who made great strides in the development of alternating current, Thomas Alva Edison, and George Westinghouse, who was Edison's rival in the "war of the currents."

Pivotal to the surge in demand for electricity was the invention of the light bulb. This was a product that many attempted to create. Early attempts include the work of Humphry Davy, who created a short-lived incandescent light bulb in 1802 by passing current through a thin strip of platinum. Edison begun to work on an electric light bulb much later, in 1878, and together with his team found that carbon filaments sealed in a vacuum lasted much longer than the other filaments they tried. Yet the defining design of the light bulb did not come until 1904, when the Hungarian Sándor Just and the Croatian Franjo Hanaman patented the use of the tungsten filament that would go on to illuminate the world.

The invention of the light bulb, the electric motor, and other essential technologies led to an explosion of the practical uses of electricity. Vacuum cleaners, refrigerators, televisions, radios, blenders, blow dryers, washing machines, dishwashers, water heaters, and certainly public lighting and industrial machines transformed our society in a matter of decades. We now generate more than twenty million gigawatt-hours of electricity every year.[9] This is enough electricity to send Marty McFly back into the future millions of times, or enough to run a 100-watt electric bulb for 22.8 billion years, which is roughly twice the age of the universe.

So what has any of this to do with Chile? The only connection between Chile and the history of electricity comes from the fact that the Atacama Desert is full of copper atoms, which, just like most Chileans, were utterly unaware of the electric dreams that powered the passion of Faraday and Tesla. As the inventions that made these atoms valuable were created, Chile retained the right to hold many of these atoms hostage. Now Chile can make a living out of them.

This brings us back to the narrative of exploitation we described earlier. The idea of crystallized imagination should make it clear that Chile is the one exploiting the imagination of Faraday, Tesla, and others, since it was the inventors' imagination that endowed copper atoms with economic value.

But Chile is not the only country that exploits foreign creativity this way. Oil producers like Venezuela and Russia exploit the imagination of Henry Ford, Rudolf Diesel, Gottlieb Daimler, Nicolas Carnot, James Watt, and James Joule by being involved in the commerce of a dark gelatinous goo that was virtually useless until combustion engines were invented.[10]

Making a strong distinction between the generation of value and the appropriation of monetary compensation helps us understand the difference between wealth and economic development. In fact, the world has many countries that are rich but still have underdeveloped economies. This is a distinction that we will explore in detail in Part IV. But making this distinction, which comes directly from the idea of crystallized imagination, helps us see that economic development is based not on the ability of a pocket of the economy to consume but on the ability of people to turn their dreams into reality. Economic development is not the ability to buy but the ability to make.

As you can probably imagine, making some crystals of imagination is not easy. To illustrate this, let's go back to the stories of Hugh and Ed. Both Hugh and Ed are creating inventions that are easy to fantasize about. These technologies are ubiquitous in movies such as *Star Wars, Terminator,* and *The Matrix,* but they are not at all ubiquitous in our world. Hugh and Ed are considered special not because they had the "idea" of robotic limbs or brain-computer interfaces but because they are carving the path through which these fantasies are becoming a reality. Fantasizing about robotic limbs is easy. Building them is hard.

Making crystals of imagination requires an enormous amount of knowledge and knowhow. Hugh and Ed are able to accumulate this knowledge and knowhow by collaborating with a brilliant entourage of colleagues and students. So while robotic limbs embody Hugh's imagination, Hugh's nervous system and those of his team members embody the knowledge and knowhow needed to transform that imagination into reality. Ultimately, it is this knowledge and knowhow that are most valuable—and are harder to accumulate.

Unfortunately, it is common for people to confuse the value of products with the value of the knowledge and knowhow needed to make them, or to confuse knowledge and knowhow with ideas. Separating the latter two is easy: I have just told you about the idea of making robotic legs, but I am pretty sure you do not know how to make them. To illustrate the difference between the value of knowledge and knowhow and the value of the products that are the fruit of knowledge and knowhow, I will borrow another story from my colleagues, one that Nicholas Negroponte, the founder of the MIT Media Lab, shared with us in a faculty meeting.

This is the story of Kelvin Doe. Kelvin is a young man from Sierra Leone who built a radio and batteries using scrap materials. Certainly many people were excited about Kelvin's engineering skills, and they should be. As a way to honor his skills, Kelvin was invited to the MIT Media Lab, where he participated in MIT's Visiting Practitioners Program. At the end of the program, Nicholas asked him about his future plans. Enthusiastically, Kelvin told Nicholas that he planned to go back to Sierra Leone to build a battery factory. Here is where Nicholas suddenly paused in his narrative. Raising his voice in a controlled manner, he said, "This is exactly the opposite of what he should do!"

In retrospect, it is easy to understand Nicholas' point. Kelvin's batteries were cool, but they were also infinitely inferior to the batteries produced by the world's leading battery manufacturers. Kelvin, despite his brilliance, mistook the value of the battery he made, and which brought him fame, for the value of having the ability to make a battery out of scrap. It was the latter that needed to be nurtured. It was the ability to *make* that was truly valuable. Kelvin's batteries were cool, but Kelvin was cooler. After all, batteries are commercially accessible anywhere. Kids who can figure out how to build batteries out of scrap are not.

Thinking about products as crystals of imagination helps us understand the importance of the source of the information that is embodied in a product. Complex products are not just arrangements of atoms that perform functions; rather, they are ordered arrangements of atoms that originated as imagination. In some cases, this metaphor is quite literal. Nikola Tesla said that he could imagine machines fully before he constructed them. According to him, his imagination was such that he did not have to tinker with prototypes and models after he had formed the plans of the machine fully within his mind.[11] Even though most of us are not as cool as Tesla, we still engage in the production of items that are the fruit of our imagination. We crystallize imagination when we write, cook, and doodle, and if we are anything like Hugh, Ed, and Kelvin, we also get to crystallize imagination when we invent.

But to fully understand the economic value of a product we need to go beyond its physical order and its origins, and incorporate information about the context in which this physical order is used. The arrangements of atoms or electrons we know as products are not just ordered; they involve orders that help us perform specific functions. In the case of Hugh's leg, the functions involve walking and running. In the case of Ed's brain-machine interfaces, the functions have yet to be decided on. Yet the ability of a product to perform functions is intimately connected to both the arrangements we equate with order or information and the context in which these are used. To understand the connection between order and functions, consider a library. In a library we can arrange books by title, topic, publication year, size, or language. Each of these orders contains information, but the information embodied in each order facilitates different functions. In the case of the library these are search functions. For instance, ordering books by topic and publication year can help us quickly identify the earliest books on quantum mechanics. Ordering books by their author's last name can help us quickly find all of the works of Mark Twain; furthermore, this is true whether we order books in alphabetical order or in reverse alphabetical order, telling us that alphabetical order and reverse alphabetical order are equivalent, at least with respect to the search function they help perform.

A less abstract example illustrating the importance of context for a product's use is a medicinal pill. Medicinal pills embody little information, as their active compound is usually a small and relatively simple molecule. Yet medicinal pills can be extremely useful and valuable. Why? To understand the value of a pill we need to understand both the context in which this information was produced and the context in which this information is used. Implicit in a pill we have the practical uses of the knowledge, imagination, and knowhow of its creators. The creators of the pill were able to identify the biological impact of that small chemical compound, and while the knowledge of how they achieved this is not embodied in the pill, its practical uses are present implicitly in the context in which the pill is used. Also, the makers of the pill had to figure out how to synthesize it, implying that the pill, while simple at the end, was the output of a process rich in the use and processing of knowledge, knowhow, and information. A pill is valuable because of this context, which involves the knowledge, knowhow, and information embodied in the environment in which the pill is used and produced, rather than the pill itself.

It is the idea of context that will help us understand the value of products as intermediaries of information, but more importantly, as intermediaries of the practical uses of knowledge and knowhow. In the next chapter we will explore why products are useful, in an attempt to answer the question: why humans bother to make tangible instantiations of their imagination. As we will see, it cannot be just because we are able to do so, but also it cannot be because of either greed or self-interest.[12] After all, crocodiles and zebras are not unable to build complex societies because of a lack of greed or self-interest. So the next stop in our journey will explore why we make products, that is, why we have a tireless commitment to transform dreams into reality.

5

Amplifiers

We don't make most of the food we eat, we don't grow it, anyway. We wear clothes other people make, we speak a language other people developed, we use a mathematics other people evolved and spent their lives building. I mean we're constantly taking things. It's a wonderful ecstatic feeling to create something and put it into the pool of human experience and knowledge.

—STEVE JOBS

In my talks, I often ask the attendees to raise their hands if they have used toothpaste that morning. I find this to be a good way to get audience participation, since the embarrassment of not having used toothpaste encourages even the shyest attendee to raise her hand. After almost everyone has raised a hand and I crack a joke about those who didn't, I ask audience members to keep their hands up only if they know how to synthesize sodium fluoride. As you can imagine, all hands go down. This shows that products give us access not only to embodied information but also to the practical uses of the knowledge that is required to make them. That is, products give us access to the practical uses of the knowledge and knowhow residing in the nervous systems of other people.

In this chapter I will discuss the practical applications of our ability to crystallize imagination. These include the ability of products to distribute the practical uses of the knowledge and knowhow used in their production, but also products as a means of creative expression, human augmentation, and combinatorial creativity.

Going back to our toothpaste example, we can note that when we are buying toothpaste we are not simply buying paste in a tube. Instead, we are buying access to the practical uses of the creativity of the person who invented toothpaste, the scientific knowledge informing the chemical synthesis that is required to make toothpaste, the knowhow required to synthesize sodium fluoride, put it inside a tube, and make it available across the planet, and the knowledge that fluoride makes our teeth stronger and has beneficial effects on our health. Something as simple as toothpaste gives us indirect access to the practical uses of the imagination, knowledge, and knowhow that exist, or existed, in the nervous systems of people we have probably never met.

The ability of toothpaste to provide us with access to the practical uses of the knowledge and knowhow embodied in a stranger's nervous system is quite magical. Yet the magic of toothpaste, much like that of any product, does not reside solely in this ability. Products are magical also because they endow us with capacities that transcend our individual limits. Products augment us, and this is a great reason why we want them.

Think of a guitar. Guitars allow us to "sing" with our hands by combining knowledge of the Pythagorean scale with expertise about the right wood for building a guitar and how to shape it. If the guitar is electric, it will also embody knowledge of how the music's sound waves can be captured using a transducer, and how these sounds can be amplified for many of us to enjoy. All of these are capacities that are needed to make music, at least the kind of music that requires a loud electric guitar. Yet these do not need to be capacities of the musician. The musician accesses the practical uses of this knowledge through the guitar, and in doing so, he is augmented by being endowed with the capacity to sing with his hands.

Products are magical largely because they augment our capacities. Planes endow us with the ability to fly, ovens with the ability to cook, and toothpaste with the ability to keep our teeth until old age. So a good reason for humans to desire products is that products augment our capacities by providing us with access to the practical uses of the knowledge and knowhow that is embodied in the nervous system of other people. Yet our need to create complex products is not only practical. We also should consider the expressive component in the creation of products (even though this expressive component is, ironically, repressed in many people). We also crystallize imagination because this allows us to transform our ideas into a *sharable* reality. It is not only through consumption that we satisfy our hedonism. We want others to like us, to want us, and to feel the way we do. We want others to know what it feels like to see the world from our perspective. Reembodying our thoughts into objects is a great way of achieving exactly that, as anyone who takes the word *inspiration* seriously has found.

Crystallizing our thoughts into tangible and digital objects is what allows us to share our thoughts with others. Otherwise, our thoughts are trapped in the prison of our minds. A musician records her music as a way to perfect her art, but also as a way of creating copies of her mind that can be shared with others and that can survive her. Without these copies her talents would be trapped in her body, inaccessible to others. We crystallize imagination to make copies of our thoughts and share them with others. This makes crystallizing imagination the essence of creative expression.

But does this mean that products are simply a form of communication? Not so fast. Our ability to crystallize imagination into products, although expressive, is different from our ability to verbally articulate ideas. An important difference is that products can augment our capacities in ways that narrative descriptions cannot. Talking about toothpaste does not help you clean your teeth, just as talking about the chemistry of gasoline will not fill up your car with gas. It is the toothpaste's embodiment of the practical uses of knowledge, knowhow, and imagination, not a narrative description of them, that endows other people with those practical uses. Without this physical embodiment the practical uses of knowledge and knowhow cannot be transmitted. Crystallizing imagination is therefore essential for sharing the practical uses of the knowledge that we accumulate in our mind. Without our ability to crystallize imagination, the practical uses of knowledge would not exist, because that practicality does not reside solely in the idea but hinges on the tangibility of the implementation. Once again, the physicality of products—whether tangible or digital— *augments us.* And it is through this augmentation that products help us communicate something that words cannot: the practical uses of knowhow, imagination, and knowledge.

Emphasizing the ability of products to augment human capacities can help us refine what we understand as the economy. It helps us see the economy not as the careful management of resources, the wealth of a nation, or a network of financial transactions, but as a system that amplifies the practical uses of knowledge and knowhow through the physical embodiment of information and the context-specific properties that this information helps carry. This is an interpretation of the economy as a *knowledge and know-how amplifier,* or a *knowledge and knowhow amplification engine*: a complex sociotechnical system able to produce physical packages containing the information needed to augment the humans who participate in it.[1] Ultimately, the economy is the collective system by which humans make information grow.

Emphasizing the ability of products to augment human capacities can also help us refine our understanding of wealth. The augmentation that is provided by our ability to pack the practical uses of knowledge as information is what allows people to live at comfort levels that are much higher than they would be able to sustain in isolation. This provides an important connection between the comforts that we associate with wealth and our species' ability to augment its capacities. Without the ability of the economy to amplify knowledge and imagination, our lives would be no different from those of other animals, or that of a castaway on a deserted island. Our ability to crystallize imagination teaches us an important lesson about the complexity of economies: markets do not make us richer but *wiser*, since they produce wealth as long as they give us indirect access to the practical uses of the knowledge and imagination that our species has been able to accumulate.

To illustrate the knowledge amplification powers of the economy, consider the nineteenth-century physicist Michael Faraday. Among other things, Faraday developed the laws of induction that are central to the generation of electricity. Yet Faraday also got his hands dirty and crystallized his ideas by embodying them in practical objects. Faraday is credited with the invention of the electric motor, which was later perfected by Tesla. So when we blow-dry our hair, vacuum our floors, or make a daiquiri in a blender, we are receiving a favor from none other than Michael Faraday, someone whom we, our parents, and even our grandparents are unlikely to have met.

The economy is the system that amplified the practical uses of the knowledge that was developed and accumulated in Faraday's brain—and which was inspired in part by Ada Lovelace.[2] Faraday's ghost, therefore, lives in all electrical products, together with those of Lovelace, Tesla, Edison, Maxwell, and many other great scientists whom we know only through their work. Ultimately, the world of products is more social than what we would naively imagine, and in a deep metaphorical sense it is a world that is populated densely by ghosts. These ghosts are the information begotten by others that survives embodied in objects, and also in us.

So our ability to crystallize imagination benefits our species for three main reasons. First, it helps us create a society of "phony geniuses," a society in which the capacities of individuals greatly surpass their individual knowledge. This is the direct result of the augmentation that is enabled by our ability to embody knowledge in tangible and digital gadgets. Second, crystallizing imagination is essential if we are to share the practical uses of our knowledge with others. Without our ability to crystallize imagination, there would be almost no creative outlets, and the practical uses of our knowledge would be trapped in the prison of our minds. Finally, the augmentation provided by products helps liberate people's search for new forms of expression and gives rise to new capacities. This is the combinatorial creativity that emerges from our species' ability to crystallize imagination. If Jimmy Page had to mine metals and build his own guitars, we would probably have not been able to enjoy "Stairway to Heaven." If Ernest Hemingway had to construct his own pens, manufacture paper, and invent the printing press, he probably would not have been able to write *The Old Man and the Sea*. By the same token, if I had to build my own laptop, you would not be reading this book. So the knowledge amplification powers of the economy are essential to liberate the creative capacities that allow our species to create new products— which continue to augment us—and endow us with new forms of artistic expression.

Our capacity to create products that augment us also helps define the overall complexity of our society. To illustrate this seemingly far-fetched connection, I will move our gaze away from humans and consider instead ant colonies, an example suggested by Norbert Wiener in his 1950 book *The Human Use of Human Beings*.[3]

Norbert Wiener, the father of cybernetics, understood that the ability to embody information outside our bodies is not unique to our species. In fact, our ability to print information in our environment makes us similar to other eusocial species, such as ants. Single ants are not very clever, but their ability to deposit information in the form of pheromones can make ant colonies extremely savvy. Thanks to their ability to deposit information in their physical environment, ants can solve difficult problems of transportation, construction, ventilation, and routing. Humans have a similar capacity. Yet instead of leaving behind pheromones, we leave behind physical instantiations of imaginary objects, such as wrenches, screwdrivers, dishwashers, pyramids, chairs, and beer bottles. The ability to deposit imaginary information in our environment is key for our species' ability to create societies and economies that are significantly more complex than those of ants. Unlike ants, we embody information not just to communicate but also to augment one another's capacities by making available—through objects— the practical uses of knowledge, knowhow, and imagination.

*   *   *

Now that we have described products as physical embodiments of information, carrying the practical uses of knowledge, knowhow, and imagination, we will move on to explore the factors that limit people's ability to make products. As we will see, the constraints limiting people's ability to accumulate the knowledge and knowhow necessary to make products are what makes the growth of information in the economy both unequal and challenging.

PART III

The Quantization of Knowhow

In 2013 Josep Guardiola, the former coach of Barcelona and current coach of Bayern Munich, visited the MIT Media Lab. Guardiola—or Pep, as he is informally known—had accepted an invitation to visit MIT from his friend and MIT's treasurer, Israel Ruiz. After some emails involving Israel, Joi Ito, and me, I was put in charge of preparing for Pep's visit, a responsibility that I accepted happily.

Pep's visit was easy to organize. Students from my group and other groups at the Media Lab were excited to present their work to the soccer celebrity. Yet, since students from other departments also wanted to meet him, I decided to organize a short Q&A session. It was in this Q&A that a student asked, "Pep, if we built a team of robots, would you come and coach it?" His reply was short and cunning. He said, and I paraphrase: "The main challenge of coaching a team is not figuring out a game plan, but getting that game plan into the heads of the players. Since in the case of robots I do not see that as a challenge, I kindly decline your offer."

Pep's answer summarized succinctly one of the main challenges of working with teams of humans. His years of coaching experience had taught him that one of the most difficult aspects of his work was not just figuring out a game plan but distributing the plan among his players. Pep's challenge was not simply one of communication—after all, it is clear that he was not interested in having players merely recite his game plan. He wanted players to be able to *act* according to his plan in the heat of the game. The plan had to be deeply internalized, and that embodiment was what made coaching challenging.

Pep's problem involves physical embodiment, although in this case it involved embodying knowledge and knowhow in players, not just information in atoms. Just as products are made of matter and information, sports teams—and firms and musical groups—are made of people who embody knowhow and knowledge. Knowhow and knowledge are embodied in the nervous systems of the soccer players, but also in the team as a whole, since players need to process information collectively to coordinate offensive maneuvers and repel attacks. The knowledge and knowhow embodied in a soccer team, however, hinge largely on the team's diversity, since goalies and strikers (much like drummers and guitar players in a band, or like quarterbacks and offensive linemen on a football team) differ in the individual knowhow they possess. This means that players contribute to the team by adding knowledge and knowhow that is not entirely redundant with that of others. This diversity is what allows teams to perform actions that cannot be achieved by single individuals, whether it's the actions needed by a soccer team to win a game or those needed by an orchestra to play one of Beethoven's symphonies. This division of knowledge and knowhow, not just labor, is what endows networks of people with fantastic capacities, such as those required by soccer teams to win the Champions League. Yet, as we will see in this chapter and in the next ones, accumulating knowledge and knowhow in a network of people is not easy. Ultimately, it is this challenge that makes the growth of information difficult and the problem of economic development hard.

As we will see in the next pages, the challenge of economic development is constrained not only by the duality between matter and information but also by the duality between systems and computation. In society, the latter is the duality between networks of people and their capacity to process information, which we know as knowledge and knowhow.

Economic systems, just like all natural systems, have an ability to produce information that is constrained by the systems' computational capacity. For information to grow in the economy, the computational capacity of the economy needs to grow as well. Increasing the computational capacity of economic systems, however, is not easy, since the growth of an economy's computational capacity is constrained by the ability of people to embody knowledge and knowhow in networks of people. So to understand the growth of information in the economy we need to understand the mechanisms that limit people's ability to form the networks they need to accumulate volumes of knowledge and knowhow that transcend a person's individual capacity. I will dedicate the next three chapters of this book to describe the challenges that limit our ability to form networks, and to embody knowledge and knowhow in the networks of people that make information grow.

6

This Time, It's Personal

Thanks to our ability to crystallize imagination, our standard of living continues to rise. Our ability to crystallize imagination is what endows us with the capacity to read at night, refrigerate our fresh fruits and vegetables, search among trillions of online documents, and travel around the world in less than a day. Yet our ability to create the complex products that endow us with these fantastic capacities is spread unevenly across the globe. Our world is populated by a myriad of products that only a few countries and regions know how to make. Our ability to crystallize imagination is geographically speckled, but why? Why is our ability to create refrigerators, jet engines, and memory devices concentrated in a few parts of the world? Why do many countries know how to make and export shoes but only a few know how to make and export helicopters? What underlies these contrasts?[1] The simple answer to this question is that developing the ability to create each crystal of imagination is difficult, and before countries can enter a market, they need to figure out how to make the goods that are transacted in that market.[2]

This figuring-out step is crucial, since overly optimistic economic models have often assumed that demand and incentives are enough to stimulate the production of any product. Incentives work to motivate intermediaries and traders, but makers, who are the ones that provide the substance of what is traded, need more than an incentive to make something. They need to know how to do it.

The truth is that making products in the real world is difficult because it requires knowhow and knowledge. So to understand why our ability to crystallize imagination is spread unevenly across the globe, we need to understand why it is difficult to accumulate the knowledge and knowhow required to create complex products.

As we discussed previously, complex products embody and amplify the practical uses of knowledge and knowhow. Hence, the people making these products need to have access to the knowledge and knowhow required to make them in their "raw" form—that is, the knowledge and knowhow embodied in human flesh, not the practical uses of knowledge and knowhow embodied implicitly in items. In academic circles this humanly embodied knowledge is referred to as "tacit" knowledge when it involves knowhow that cannot be explicitly described. As the Hungarian polymath Michael Polanyi cleverly noted, often "we know more than we can tell."[3]

The separation between the practical uses of knowledge and knowhow and the knowledge and knowhow embodied in people implies that making products will be more difficult in the places where obtaining access to people with specific forms of knowledge and knowhow is more difficult. If knowledge and knowhow were easy to accumulate, people could easily acquire whatever knowhow they needed to make the crystals of imagination they don't yet know how to make. In that world, it would be relatively easy for any group of people to start making any product, and therefore differences in the ability of countries to make products should be small or nonexistent. Yet in a world where knowledge and knowhow are trapped in social networks and are difficult to copy, we should expect large differences in countries' abilities to crystallize imagination, since differences in the knowledge and knowhow available in a given country should be reflected in the set of products that each country is able to produce.

But how difficult is it to accumulate knowledge and knowhow? All evidence points to the fact that our world is one in which knowledge and knowhow are "heavier" than the atoms we use to embody their practical uses. Information can be moved around easily in the products that contain it, whether these are objects, books, or webpages, but knowledge and knowhow are trapped in the bodies of people and the networks that these people form. Knowledge and knowhow are so "heavy" that when it comes to a simple product such as a cellphone battery, it is infinitely easier to bring the lithium atoms that lie dormant in the Atacama Desert to Korea than to bring the knowledge of lithium batteries that resides in Korean scientists to the bodies of the miners who populate the Atacaman cities of Antofagasta and Calama. Our world is marked by great international differences in countries' ability to crystallize imagination. These differences emerge because countries differ in the knowledge and knowhow that are embodied in their populations, and because accumulating knowledge and knowhow in people is difficult. But why is it hard for us to accumulate the knowledge and knowhow we need to transform our dreams into reality?

At the individual level, accumulating knowledge is difficult because learning is experiential. That is, we accumulate knowledge and knowhow mostly through practice, such as on-the-job experience. This idea, that of learning being experiential, has a long tradition in the social sciences and economics. As the educator and sociologist Walter Powell puts it: "There are a number of jobs that are based, in large measure, on either intellectual capital or craft-based skills, both of which have been honed through years of education, training and experience. Many of these kinds of knowledge-intensive activities, such as cultural production, scientific research, design work, mathematical analysis, computer

programming or software development, and some professional services, require little in the way of costly peripheral resources. They
are based on knowhow and detailed knowledge of the abilities of
others who possess similar or complementary skills. Knowhow typ-
ically involves a kind of tacit knowledge that is difficult to codify."[4]

To grab on to the tacitness of knowledge or knowhow and its relevance for economic life, imagine that you are organizing an event
and need to hire a musician. If books contained the knowhow that
products and services crystallize, then you could solve your problem by picking up any random person from the street and giving
him or her a guitar and some sheet music. Although such a show
may be entertaining, the chances are that the entertainment will
not be very musical. Hiring a musician by picking up a random
person from the street is a bad idea because even though the information available in books can help us speed up the accumulation of knowledge and knowhow, knowledge and knowhow are not
present in books. For instance, a book can tell us how to position
our bodies for karate moves. But I would not recommend that you
jump into the ring of an ultimate fighting event if your only fighting experience comes from reading some karate books. Knowhow,
in particular, resides primarily in humans' nervous systems. It is
the instinctive way in which the musician plays guitar, the fluidity
with which the artist draws, and the dexterity with which the truck
driver backs up an eighteen-wheeler. It is not in books.

Getting knowledge inside a human's nervous system is not easy
because learning is both experiential and social.[5] To say that learning is social means that people learn from people: children learn
from their parents and employees learn from their coworkers (I
hope). The social nature of learning makes the accumulation of
knowledge and knowhow geographically biased. People learn from
people, and it is easier for people to learn from others who are
experienced in the tasks they want to learn than from people with
no relevant experience in that task. For instance, it is difficult to

become an air traffic controller without learning the trade from other air traffic controllers, just as it is difficult to become a surgeon without having ever been an intern or a resident at a hospital. By the same token, it is hard to accumulate the knowhow needed to manufacture rubber tires or an electric circuit without interacting with people who have made tires or circuits.[6] Ultimately, the experiential and social nature of learning not only limits the knowledge and knowhow that individuals can achieve but also biases the accumulation of knowledge and knowhow toward what is already available in the places where these individuals reside. This implies that the accumulation of knowledge and knowhow is geographically biased.

The social and experiential aspects of learning imply that there is a limit to the amount of knowledge and knowhow an individual can accumulate. That limit makes the accumulation of knowledge and knowhow at the collective level even more difficult, because such an accumulation requires that we break up knowledge and knowhow into chunks that are smaller than the ones an individual can hold.

Chopping up knowhow compounds the difficulties involved in individuals' accumulation of knowhow not only because it multiplies the problem of accumulating knowledge and knowhow by the number of individuals involved but also because it introduces the combinatorial problem of connecting individuals in a structure that can reconstitute the knowledge and knowhow that were chopped up in the first place. That structure is a network. Our collective ability to accumulate knowledge is therefore limited by both the finite capacity of individuals, which forces us to chop up large volumes of knowledge and knowhow, and the problem of connecting individuals in a network that can put this knowledge and knowhow back together.

We can simplify this discussion by defining the maximum amount of knowledge and knowhow that a human nervous system can accumulate as a fundamental unit of measurement. We call this unit a *personbyte*, and define it as the maximum knowledge and knowhow carrying capacity of a human.

Personbytes are fundamental in the sense that the accumulation of a volume of knowledge and knowhow that is smaller than a personbyte is constrained only by individual limitations (including experience and social learning), whereas the accumulation of an amount of knowledge and knowhow that is larger than a personbyte is also constrained by collective limitations (including chunking up and distributing that knowledge and knowhow).[7] If we say that an individual can hold up to one personbyte of knowledge and knowhow, then all products that require more than one personbyte of knowledge and knowhow to be produced will require teams of individuals. Furthermore, creating a team capable of making a complex product requires accumulating the knowledge and knowhow in the context of a relatively harmonious social network.

To illustrate the difference between accumulating small volumes of productive knowledge and knowhow (less than one personbyte) and larger volumes (many personbytes), let's return to our music example and consider a band instead of a musician. If hiring a random person from the street was a bad approach for getting a musician, hiring a bunch of strangers is probably a worse approach for getting a band, since a band's performance adds a layer of complexity that is absent in the performance of a single musician. A successful band not only requires each musician to have a deep knowledge of his or her instrument but also requires musicians to know how to play together. As Pep knew was the case for a soccer team, a band is a network whose success requires a deep connection among its members, since a performance involves not simply combining sounds but beautifully weaving them together. So accumulating the knowledge and knowhow needed to have a successful band—let's say of four people—is harder than accumulating the knowledge and knowhow required for four single musicians to play individually. For example, we need to add in practice time for them to experience playing together and learn to coordinate their activities. There are also other social and economic processes that can make it difficult for people to form networks, such as the lack of a shared language or trust. I will review these social processes in the next two chapters. For the time being, however, the only thing we need to know is that when these processes increase the cost of interpersonal links they limit the ability of people to form the networks they need to accumulate knowledge and knowhow. Yet when obstacles are overcome and people do come together, the outcomes can be sublime. The difference between a network and a group of isolated individuals is the difference between the Beatles and the solo careers of their members, or the difference between the Apollo program and a collection of science and engineering graduates.[8] Putting people together does not always result in endeavors of such cultural resonance, but when it does, our species can achieve things that can make us all proud (or, in some other cases, ashamed).

* * *

We started this discussion by asking why the ability to create complex products is geographically speckled, and noted that this speckledness suggested that creating complex products is difficult. Then we explored what makes the creation of complex products problematic, and noted that creating complex products is difficult because the knowledge and knowhow needed to create them is hard to accumulate. At the individual level, the experiential and social nature of learning slows down the accumulation of knowledge and knowhow.[9] More important, though, is that it limits the total amount of knowledge and knowhow an individual can accumulate to less than one personbyte. The personbyte is therefore a quantization limit, since it represents a fundamental quantum of knowledge and knowhow over which actual knowledge and knowhow need to be subdivided. The personbyte limit implies that the accumulation of large amounts of knowledge and know-how are limited by both the individual constraints of social and experiential learning and the collective constraints brought by our need to chop up large volumes of knowledge and knowhow and distribute them in networks of individuals.

Of course, the social and experiential nature of learning does not mean that genetic factors do not play a role in our ability to accumulate knowhow (it is hard to teach a goldfish how to play the piano, even in the best social context). Studies using identical and nonidentical twins have associated genes with a number of behavioral traits.[10] These include traits that we would not naively expect to be associated with genes, such as a person's preference for a political party and likelihood of political participation.[11] Musical ability is another example of a trait that involves accumulating knowhow but is also affected by an individual's genetic makeup. Recent studies using identical and nonidentical twins have shown that genes help explain musical ability, in part because of their effect on an individual's willingness to practice an instrument and in part by affecting what we colloquially describe as talent.[12]

The fact that genetics can modulate the ability of an individual to accumulate knowhow, however, does not affect the core of our story, as the genetic diversity of most populations is large enough to ensure that differences between ethnic, national, and religious groups cannot be explained by genes, even when differences between individuals can be explained by genetic factors. The genius of Mozart, even if it is partly due to genetics, does not mean that all Austrians are musically talented or that there are no tone-deaf Austrians. So the explanatory power of genetic variation among individuals must not be used to misinterpret international differences in ability or capacity, since in large populations genetic variations have a tendency to average out.[13]

The beauty of the personbyte idea is that it does not care about the nature of the factors limiting the accumulation of knowledge and knowhow. It is only concerned with the fact that the capacity of individuals to accumulate knowhow and knowledge is finite. Once we accept that the capacity of individuals is finite, we need to accept that the only way to accumulate large volumes of knowledge and knowhow is in chunks of less than one personbyte.[14] Ultimately, this chunking makes the accumulation of large volumes of knowledge and knowhow increasingly more difficult, regardless of what caused the chunking in the first place.

But is this the end of the story? Is the personbyte limit the only fundamental threshold that forces us to quantize knowledge and knowhow and limits our ability to accumulate them? Or are there other thresholds that emerge when the amounts of knowledge and knowhow are much greater than one personbyte?

Our modern reality is the result of volumes of knowledge and knowhow vastly larger than one personbyte. So next we will explore the structures holding volumes of knowledge and knowhow that surpass the personbyte limit and even escape the knowledge and knowhow accumulation capacities of firms. This will help us understand how the accumulation of knowledge and knowhow is quantized not just by our need to embody knowledge in people but also by the networks that people form. Understanding the difficulties that quantization imposes for the accumulation of knowhow will help us understand why our ability to produce complex products is limited to a few places, and therefore help us understand the fundamental differences that separate countries at different stages of economic development.

7

Links Are Not Free

The Ford Motor Company's River Rouge complex is considered by many to be the highest expression of industrialization. When the Rouge was completed in 1927, it had ninety-three buildings totaling sixteen million square feet of factory space. This is about half of the square footage of New York's Central Park! The Rouge housed more than a hundred thousand workers and was able to take in iron ore at one end and spit out cars at the other. You might say it was the quintessential personbyte cathedral.

But why was the Rouge so damn big? Classical answers to this question involve scale economies and the division of labor. The idea of scale economies is that the per-unit cost of items decreases as we make more of them. In simple words, it is the difference between cooking dinner for one and cooking for a family of five. Certainly, cooking for five does not take five times the effort or ingredients than cooking for one. Adam Smith's division of labor, on the other hand, is one of the mechanisms that can help explain scale economies. The division of labor implies that it is more efficient to have each worker focus on a small part of the construction of a pin or a car than to have each worker attempt to build that pin or car from start to finish. But the division of labor only makes sense for projects that are large enough to make it worthwhile.

To make one pin, for example, we do not need to divide labor. To make hundreds of thousands of pins, and certainly to make hundreds of thousands of cars, we do. So the division of labor and scale economies can help us justify why Ford wanted a plant as big as River Rouge. But they cannot explain why industrial complexes of that size emerged to manufacture cars but not to make pins. To explain the differences in size between pin factories and car factories we need to bring in an additional assumption. This additional assumption is the quantization of knowledge and knowhow, since this implies that larger networks are needed to hold the knowledge and knowhow required to make cars than that needed to make pins.

Certainly we are not implying that a car plant requires a number of personbytes that is equal to the number of people employed in a car factory or to the number of tasks that are executed by all workers. Rather, we can say that the number of people employed in a car factory is a generous upper limit of the number of personbytes needed to make a car. Henry Ford divided the production of the Model T into increasingly smaller tasks—7,882, to be precise.[1] The number of tasks needed to make a Model T is larger than the number of tasks required to produce a pin, but that does not mean that making a Model T requires 7,882 personbytes of knowhow. A simple interpretation is that 7,882 personbytes of knowhow is a very generous upper bound for the amount of knowhow needed to produce a car from its basic ingredients: iron, soybeans, rubber, and imagination.[2]

The number of tasks involved in creating a car in the Rouge is an upper bound for the number of personbytes needed to make a car because many of these tasks are simple enough that the same individual can be an expert in a number of them. Moreover, when tasks are related to each other, the knowledge and knowhow accrued for one task will be reusable in other tasks. Using our musician example, we can say that someone who knows how to play the guitar can more easily learn how to play the ukulele. So a proper count of the personbytes accumulated in a network of people needs to subtract overlaps of knowledge held by multiple individuals. Installing the headlights and the taillights of a car are two different tasks, but performing both tasks does not require doubling the knowledge and knowhow needed to perform just one of them.

There are other factors affecting the size of productive networks. The personbyte theory implies that larger networks are needed to accumulate larger volumes of knowledge and knowhow, but it does not explicitly tell us why our world is not filled with megafactories that are ten to twenty times larger than River Rouge. After all, hasn't the complexity of products increased vastly since Ford introduced the Model T? The limited proliferation of megafactories like the Rouge implies that there must be mechanisms that limit the size of the networks we call firms and make it preferable to disaggregate production into networks of firms. This also suggests the existence of a second quantization limit, which we will call the *firmbyte*. It is analogous to the personbyte, but instead of requiring the distribution of knowledge and knowhow among people, it requires them to be distributed among a network of firms.[3]

The factors that limit the size of firms—and imply a second quantization threshold—have been studied extensively in a branch of the academic literature known as transaction cost theory or new institutional economics. Additionally, the factors that limit the size of the networks humans form—whether firms or not—have been studied extensively by the sociologists, political scientists, and economists working on social capital and social networks. Since this is an extensive literature, I will review the basics of the new institutional economics in this chapter and leave the discussion of social capital theories for the next chapter.

Transaction cost theory, or new institutional economics, is the branch of economics that studies the costs of transactions and the institutions that people develop to govern them. In simpler terms, it is the branch studying the cost of economic links and the ways in which people organize to deal with commercial interactions.

The origins of transaction cost theory can be traced back to a 1937 paper by Ronald Coase, "The Nature of the Firm."[4] As a young scholar, Coase realized that the descriptions of the economy that were prevalent at the time tended to overlook one aspect of the economy that seemed obvious to him: the fact that economic transactions are costly. As a student at the London School of Economics, Coase attended a seminar organized by Arnold Plant, who had been recently appointed as a professor of commerce.[5] It was there that Coase heard a description of the economy that contradicted his intuition and would accompany his thoughts throughout his life. This was a quote from Sir Arthur Salter: "The normal economic system works itself out."

Paraphrasing Einstein, we can say that Coase saw in Salter's quote a description of the economy that was not simple, but simpler.[6] In his landmark 1937 paper Coase noted that economies involve plenty of planning that is not coordinated by the price system and that takes place primarily within the boundaries of a firm. He noted that descriptions of the economy overlooked obvious aspects, such as the fact that workers who relocate from one department to another within a company are responding not to the price system but to the orders of a manager, or that drafting and executing contracts often involves an awful lot of work. Coase noted that economic transactions were not easy, and that the economy was not as fluid as many of his colleagues liked to assume.

In Coase's view, the economy was not a collection of fluid and frictionless market transactions but a set of islands of conscious power, shielded from each other and from the dynamics of the price mechanisms. Firms are hierarchical, Coase emphasized, and the interactions between a firm's workers are often political. So in

Coase's view, hiring a worker was a form of contract in which a person was hired to do a task that had not yet been specified, since what a worker will be asked to do a few months down the road is rarely known when she is hired. Coase dedicated much of his academic career to explaining the existence and boundaries of these islands of power. His answers become known as the transaction cost theory of the firm.

Coase's explanation of the boundaries of a firm was brilliant and simple. It was based on the idea that economic transactions are costly and not as fluid as the cheerleaders of the price mechanism religiously believed. Often, market transactions require negotiations, drafting of contracts, setting up inspections, settling disputes, and so on. These transaction costs can help us understand the boundary of the firm, since according to Coase, a parsimonious way of understanding the islands of central planning that we know as firms is to search for the point at which the cost of transactions taking place internally within the firm equals the cost of market transactions. When the external transactions become less costly than the internal transactions, firms stop growing, since it is better for them to buy things from the market than to produce these internally.

The minimalist version of Coase's theory that I present here helps us understand that there are fundamental forces that limit the size of the networks we know as firms, and hence that there is a limit to the knowledge and knowhow these networks can accumulate.[7] Moreover, it also tells us that there is a fundamental relationship between the cost of the links and the size of these networks: the cheaper the link, the larger the network.

More importantly, the limited size of firms tells us that volumes of knowledge that are larger than the networks we can form need to be shared across networks of firms. Hence, Coase helps us explain why plants like River Rouge have not taken over the world.

An example of a product that is produced by a network of firms, rather than by a single company, is the personal computer. While personal computers tend to have an identifiable brand, different firms design and manufacture different parts of a finished computer. Even Apple's devices, which are proudly designed in California, contain parts—such as their displays—that are designed and manufactured by others, including Apple's nemesis, Samsung.[8] In fact, soon after Steve Jobs returned to Apple he begun to outsource the manufacturing of devices, relying heavily on technologies from other firms.[9] The iPod was made possible by a small hard drive that was invented by Toshiba. The Gorilla Glass screen of the iPhone was the brainchild of Corning, a glass manufacturer in upstate New York. What is true for Apple products is also true for many other modern devices. In fact, no matter what brand your computer is, it is probably a salad of electronics: powered by a chip made by Intel or AMD; a hard drive made by Quantum, Samsung, Seagate, or Fujitsu; a memory made by Kingston, Corsair, or PNY; and a network card made by D-Link, TP-Link, or Netgear. All of these brands and companies are likely to be different from the one that slapped a logo on your machine, showing that computers are constructed by networks of firms rather than firms.

Yet the network of firms involved in a computer is much larger than what we have described so far. While some computers carry the same brand as their operating system (namely, Macs), the application software that makes computers fun and useful comes from a variety of other firms, from large companies such as Adobe or small indie game studios such as the ones that create cool games like Blek, Machinarium, or World of Goo.[10] Finally, many of us use computers to access the Internet, so at the end of the day this salad of software and hardware becomes a simple prerequisite for visiting social networking sites such as Facebook or Twitter, reading articles in the *New York Times,* or playing massively multiplayer online games such as World of Warcraft.

The contrast between the vast volumes of knowledge and know-how needed to make the world's most complex products and the limited knowhow carrying capacities of firms explains why we broke the firmbyte limit and why networks of firms are needed to make complex products. Yet they do not tell us whether the process of accumulating large volumes of knowledge and knowhow becomes harder once we cross the firmbyte threshold.

Coase's intuition tells us that the ability of networks of firms to hold knowledge and knowhow will depend on the cost of links. That is, when making and sustaining links is inexpensive, creating large networks of firms will be easier, and accumulating vast volumes of knowledge and knowhow will be easier, too. When links are expensive, on the other hand, it will be harder to connect firms, and so it will be harder to create the networks of firms and people needed to accumulate vast volumes of knowledge and knowhow. In short, when links are costly, our world becomes fragmented. So to answer the question of whether networks of firms facilitate or hinder the accumulation of large volumes of knowledge and knowhow, we need to learn more about the cost of firm-to-firm links.

The problem we face in this line of argument is that there are many ways in which two firms can interact. Hence talking about firm interactions in general is an oversimplification. Some firm-to-firm interactions are simple, such as ordering ink cartridges from a catalog, while others are incredibly complex, such as developing a partnership for the construction of a new manufacturing plant. Moreover, many firm interactions are embedded in social networks, which is a fact that we will consider in the next chapter. So talking about the cost of links is not simple, and it makes sense only when we define links narrowly enough.

Oliver Williamson, a student of Ronald Coase, understood that commercial links come in different sizes. He wrote extensively about the connection between the cost of firm-to-firm interactions and the institutions that people develop to manage these links.[11] Williamson's classification of links is based on two axes. On the first, he separated transactions by frequency, into recurrent and occasional. On the second, he separated transactions by specificity, from nonspecific to idiosyncratic.[12]

To understand Williamson's parsing of the world, think about the amount of paperwork and people needed to establish a commercial link. For example, think of buying a latte at your local coffee shop. This requires very little paperwork—a receipt—and just a few seconds from the cashier and the barista. No intermediaries are required to get the task done. In Williamson's language, buying coffee is a *nonspecific recurrent* transaction. Now consider buying a house. This is a transaction that requires much more paperwork. A house is also a relatively specific buy, so the interaction will likely be catalyzed by institutions that are external to the buyer and the seller, such as the bank that is issuing the mortgage, the home inspector, the real estate agents, and the real estate lawyers. In Williamson's language, the purchase of a home is an *occasional and specific* interaction, meaning that it is an interaction that needs to be chaperoned by additional institutions. Finally, consider a long-term but highly specific deal. For instance, a garment manufacturer wishes to establish a long-term collaboration with a button manufacturer that produces very specific buttons—maybe tiny pineapple-shaped buttons in gold and silver. In Williamson's language, this is a *specific and recurrent* interaction. In such interactions, developing a relationship with the supplier is more important than the participation of external institutions.[13]

Williamson used his classification scheme to connect economic transactions with the governance structures best suited for their management. Yet in our case we are interested in classifying transactions by type, not because we want to explain the institutions involved but because we want to know the costs of the links as these affect the formation of the networks we need to accumulate knowledge and knowhow.

Following Coase's intuition, we know that cheaper links give rise to larger networks, and the personbyte theory tells us that we need larger networks to accumulate more knowledge and knowhow. Now let's add Williamson's intuition to the mix.

First, let's consider the simplest links, market interactions. These are the links that Williamson calls unspecific, such as buying a coffee, a spatula, a light bulb, or a single sheet of Plexiglas. During the last decades the cost of market transactions has fallen due to, among other things, changes in transportation and communication technologies (see Figures 5–8), so we should expect the networks composed of market links to be more fluid and dense. For instance, the inflation-adjusted cost of moving goods fell by 90 percent during the twentieth century, while the change in long-distance communications in the last three centuries took us from a world in which telegraphs were mechanical contraptions used by the French elite to pass on messages to one in which videoconferencing became a teenager's pastime.[14] With falling costs the number of long distance market links can be expected to increase, and in turn, this should increase our ability to accumulate knowledge in networks of market interactions.

The cost of market interactions was reduced directly by reductions in tariffs and by improvements in shipping and communication, but other forces, such as the emergence of standards, have also reduced the cost of market interactions.[15] Examples of standards in the computer industry include the VGA port, Wi-Fi, and the USB port. These standards allow manufacturers to create products that connect seamlessly without need for any coordination between manufacturers. In fact, the USB port was invented in a collaboration between Intel, Compaq, DEC, IBM, Microsoft, NEC, and Nortel and made available through an extremely inexpensive license,

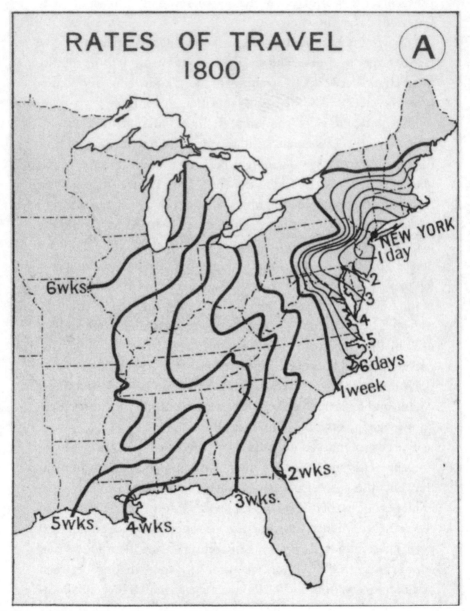

Figure 5. Rates of Travel from New York, 1800.

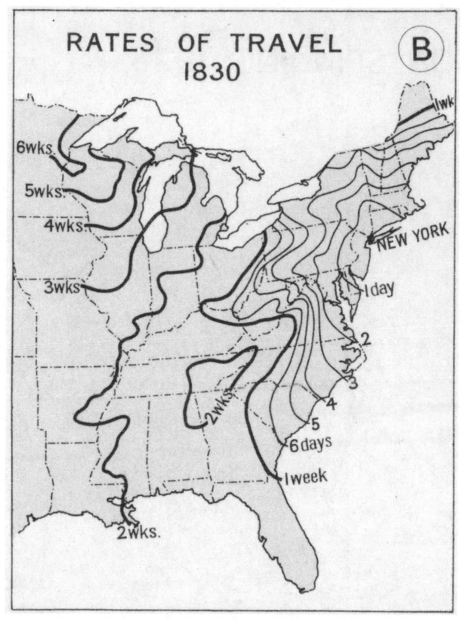

Figure 6. Rates of Travel from New York, 1830.

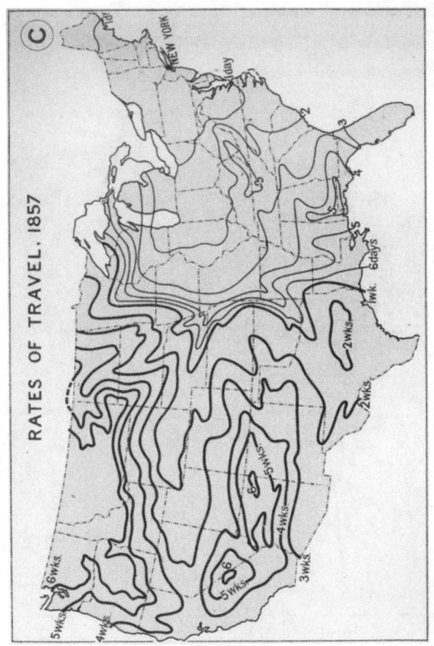

Figure 7. Rates of Travel from New York, 1857.

99

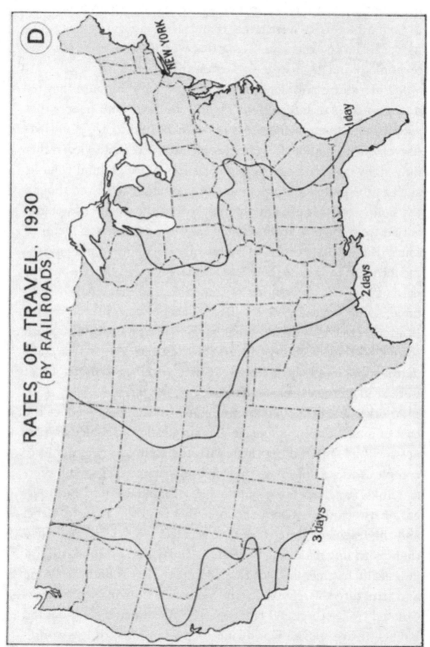

Figure 8. Rates of Travel from New York, 1930.

because these manufacturers knew that the ecosystem benefits of a standard interface were larger than the private gains they could harvest from an expensive license that would restrict access to the technology and generate a platform war.[16]

Standards are prevalent in our modern world because they reduce the costs of interactions among the firms and people that subscribe to them. Hence, it is not unexpected to see standards coevolve with markets.[17] Many people are surprised to learn that only a few centuries ago simple measures of weight and volume, such as the pound and the pint, were not standard. Even though the same word was used in different towns, the weight of a pound varied from town to town—sometimes by as much as a factor of four.[18] But as cities began to trade with one another and governments began to impose their rule over larger areas, the use of standards grew. The coevolution of standards and markets is easy to understand, since anyone buying a bushel of corn from a vendor in another town would want that bushel to mean the same in both towns. So the possibility of trade created an incentive for standardization, and helped the expansion of the governments that were keen on the use of standards.

Another example of an ancient standard that helps reduce the cost of interactions is language. Language allows people to weave networks by empowering them with the ability to communicate complex ideas, coordinate their actions, and establish commercial links. Language is the quintessential standard. It is the difference between the network of people that built the Tower of Babel and the fragmented network that was left after "God" punished them with linguistic fragmentation. Today our world is still linguistically fragmented, but that fragmentation is both declining and structured. Twelve thousand years ago, humans spoke an estimated twelve thousand languages.[19] An estimated six thousand languages are spoken worldwide today, but most of the world's population communicates in a few global languages. And in many important online and offline forums, including Twitter, Wikipedia, and book translations, English has emerged as the "hub" language bridging communication between most other languages.[20] As a Chilean married to a Russian, working with students from the United States, Israel, Bulgaria, Macedonia, Chile, Argentina, Germany, and India, I am a living example of the benefits that the existence of a global hub language such as English is able to provide.

Now let's bring this discussion back to the ability of firms to create networks that can help accumulate large volumes of knowledge and knowhow. When we narrow our focus to market links, we can say that our ability to weave denser networks of domestic and international firms has been enhanced by improvements in communication and transportation technologies and also by the proliferation of standards in both language and technology. So it is safe to conclude that the costs of narrowly defined commercial links, those that are as easy as ordering something from a catalog, have declined over the past century, and that our ability to accumulate knowledge and knowhow in the networks of firms and people based on these simple interactions has probably increased. These networks involve primarily manufacturing networks, since these manufacturing activities involve communication and exchange of intermediate products that carry the practical uses of knowledge and knowhow.

In *Managed by the Markets*, Gerald Davis describes the manufacturing of a Barbie doll. Manufacturing a Barbie doll involves a collection of processes that take place in twenty different countries.[21] If we assume that manufacturing a Barbie requires less productive knowledge than manufacturing a car (and it probably does), then we can conclude that the manufacturing was spread out not because making a Barbie doll requires more knowledge and knowhow than a firm can contain, but because the reduction in the costs of establishing international commercial links made it possible to spread out the knowledge and knowhow required to make a Barbie doll into twenty different countries.

Yet, as Coase and Williamson noted, not all interactions are this easy. Now it is time to talk about the consequences of the links that are more difficult to make. These are the links involving long-term collaborations or large projects—links that often require a large amount of paperwork and people's time to be established.

Consider two large organizations wanting to establish a research collaboration. The interaction might be ignited by the interest of two researchers who fell in love with each other's work and would like to explore the fertility of their intellectual love. The "first date," however, would not involve a cup of coffee or dinner and a movie, but signing a nondisclosure agreement. This will be followed up by the creation of a contract that will need to be approved by department heads and the legal departments of both organizations, a process that often takes months. Most likely the legal departments of each organization will have conflicting policies for intellectual property—each wants all the intellectual property for its own organization, and none for the other—and this will delay the process even further. As a result, the intellectual romance of the interaction may be lost in the negotiation of an interaction "prenup" that is more concerned about the potential of a divorce than about the fertility of the interaction. Using our shortcut to Williamson's theory, the large number of people and huge amounts of paperwork involved in this interaction tell us that it is extremely costly to make, and hence we should not expect networks that involve such highly bureaucratized interactions to hold too much knowledge and knowhow.

If you have worked in large organizations, whether in the private sector, public sector, NGO sector, or academia, you know exactly what I am talking about and will probably agree that unnecessarily bureaucratic interactions are pervasive. The simplest interactions between large organizations are hardly as fluid as picking an apple from an orchard or choosing a new printer from a catalog. In the most extreme cases, exemplified by the United Nations or many public sector organizations, external interactions are constrained by long administrative processes that require an army of administrators, extensive paperwork, and a long sequence of approvals. Sometimes this means that interactions that should be simply market transactions—such as simple forms of service procurement— wind up subject to a regime of governance that makes them far more complicated than they need to be. As a result, the bureaucratic burden involved in establishing the link is comparable to the effort required to execute the task being contracted, and the organizations effectively exclude themselves from the market they are trying to participate in. A symptom of this is the subpar provision of services in countries that have plenty of capacity; a good example is the conspicuous difference in quality and cost between the webpages of the US government and those created in Silicon Valley.

Extreme levels of inefficiency can only be supported by organizations whose revenue stream does not depend on their interactions with others, for if it did, they would have gone broke. Chief examples of these are organizations whose revenue comes from the collection of taxes, such as governments, or organizations that receive funds in a more or less unconditional way, such as the United Nations. More important, these costs affect not only the number of links but also whom these links connect to. Lengthy and cumbersome bureaucratic requirements provide an advantage to incumbents familiar with the paperwork and the people involved in their approval (known informally as "beltway bandits" in the context of the US Federal government). The people who are best at going through the paperwork, however, may not necessarily be the best people to provide the service requested.

Extreme bureaucracy generates large networks connecting many people but few personbytes. Most of the personbytes available are consumed by internal procedures, such as lengthy and politicized approval processes. As a result, such networks are weighed down by their own links, and although large, they become unable to generate or accumulate much knowhow and knowledge.

We can illustrate the costs of overbureaucratized networks by looking at a few cases, such as the health care sector in the United States. A recent survey of private US health care facilities estimated that the support staff of hospital physicians spends nineteen hours a week interacting with insurance providers in prior authorizations, while clerical staff spend thirty-six hours a week filing claims. The cost of interactions between private health care providers and private insurance providers was estimated to be $68,000 per physician per year, totaling a whopping $31 billion per year—equivalent to the GDP of the Dominican Republic in 2005.[22] The interaction costs in 1999 for the entire health care system, including private and public, were estimated on the low end to be $31 billion and on the high end to be $294 billion—which is comparable to the present day GDP of Singapore or Chile.[23] Moreover, between 1969 and 1999 the administrative cost of health care in the United States grew from 18.2 percent to 27.3 percent of the health care labor force.[24] So the costs of interaction between the health care and insurance sectors are not only high but rising.

The goal here is not to open up a discussion on the administrative costs of the US health care system but simply to highlight that interaction costs between different firms or organizations can be substantial. Ultimately, in a world in which differences in the costs of links translate into differences in connectivity of the networks of firms and organizations that beget them, the ability of the networks with the most expensive links to hold vast volumes of knowledge and knowhow will be the one that suffers.

*   *   *

We started this chapter by looking at River Rouge as a quintessential example of a personbyte cathedral. The Rouge amassed large volumes of knowledge and knowhow and produced a large number of vehicles, but it did not become the dominant model of production for the twentieth century. As the twentieth century continued to roar, networks of firms became increasingly the new norm. In the case of manufacturing, the ability of firms to interact was helped by reductions in the costs of tariffs, transportation, and communication, but also by the emergence of industry standards and the coordination enabled by hub languages. The reduction in the cost of commercial links allowed the dismemberment of manufacturing into networks of firms, as illustrated by the Barbie doll example.[25] But in other cases, such as computers, this was a condition that was also required by the limited capacity of firms to hold knowledge and knowhow. That is, the complexity of computers, which encompasses not just hardware but software and online services as well, requires the existence of networks of firms.

The complexity and finesse of modern manufactures are evidence of the increase in the ability of manufacturing networks to amass increasingly large volumes of knowledge and knowhow. Only a few centuries ago, many products were strongly associated with a few regions of the world: Champagne with France, clocks with Switzerland, Parmesan with Parma. Even though legal restrictions on the names can enforce the continuation of such associations, the point is that these associations are no longer true for many modern products. Are iPhones Californian, Chinese, or Korean? With the dismemberment of production, the nationality of products no longer makes much sense.

In addition to large volumes of knowledge and knowhow, modern manufacturing is the result of large international networks that are made of links involving the exchange of intermediate products, such as smartphone displays or the plastic pellets used to make a Barbie doll. Yet as manufacturing grew, other networks began to fold under their own weight. The cost of interactions in some sectors with large administrative burdens, such as education and health care, is high and increasing, and it is hard to argue that the increase in administrative complexity we are observing will translate into an increase in the ability of these networks to embody larger volumes of knowledge and knowhow.[26] In the case of health care, an inverse relationship between the administrative burden and the quality of care has been documented, suggesting that an excess of management and administration is not helping these networks improve their ability to put knowledge and know-how to good use.[27]

But does this mean we should attempt to make all links market links? If Coase and Williamson are right, and they are right about a few things, the diversity we observe in economic links is not a matter of choice but a fundamental characteristic of the nature of economies. The market links that we use to buy toothpaste are fundamentally different from the ones involved in long-term contracts, which, as Coase highlighted, often involve the purchase of something that is not specified at the time of the original contract. So it would be naive to think that it is possible to make all links like those we use to transact well-defined crystals of imagination, such as wineglasses and paper towels. As we will see later, adding the social dimension to these interactions will illuminate why a diversity of links is needed to form the networks that accumulate knowledge and knowhow.

Fortunately, we only need to take a few lessons from this long discussion. After all, we want to focus not on transaction costs per se but on the ability of the economy to generate structures that can hold the knowledge and knowhow required to crystallize imagination. With this goal in mind, one lesson to remember is that there is a relationship between the size of a productive network and the volume of knowledge and knowhow it can embody, with larger networks being able to embody larger volumes of knowledge and knowhow, all else being equal. Second, our ability to weave large networks depends on the costs of establishing links, with cheaper links favoring the creation of the large networks needed to amass large volumes of knowledge and knowhow.

The third lesson is that there are fundamental breaks, or transition points, in the structures of the networks that we use to accumulate knowledge and knowhow at the collective level. To amass large volumes of knowledge and knowhow we need to quantize both knowledge and knowhow, and two fundamental quanta of knowledge and knowhow were introduced for that purpose: the *personbyte*, which emerges from the finite capacity of humans, and the *firmbyte*, which emerges from the finite capacity of firms. Certainly neither personbyte nor firmbyte limits should be taken in their strict numeric sense. Both limits represent conceptual boundaries that point to important transitions in the structure of the networks needed to accumulate knowledge and knowhow, not narrowly defined thresholds. Both personbytes and firmbytes show that our ability to accumulate large volumes of knowledge and knowhow is packaged in a nested structure in which what we consider to be a network at one scale becomes a node in the next. Networks of neurons become nodes when we abstract them as people, and networks of people become nodes when we abstract them as networks of firms.

The bottom line is that accumulating large volumes of knowledge and knowhow is difficult because it requires evolving the networks that embody that knowledge and knowhow. We can think of knowledge and knowhow as continuous, but since the networks that hold them are not continuous, knowledge and knowhow must be quantized, and not just in theory but also in practice.

So the quantization of knowledge and knowhow, which is brought about in part by the cost of links, helps us answer the question of why it is difficult to accumulate increasing volumes of knowledge and knowhow. The answer is that accumulating knowledge and knowhow is difficult because creating the networks required to embody both knowledge and knowhow is difficult. But there's an important caveat. So far our explanation of the cost of links has leaned too strongly on economic arguments such as those advanced by Coase and Williamson. There are also important sociological and cultural processes that affect the structure of social networks. So in the next chapter I will review other strands of literature connecting the structure of social networks with economic outcomes.

8

In Links We Trust

A society built entirely out of rational individuals who come together on the basis of a social contract for the sake of the satisfaction of their wants cannot form a society that would be viable over any length of time.
—FRANCIS FUKUYAMA

Trust, by which I mean the confidence that others will do the "right" thing despite a clear balance of incentives to the contrary, emerges, if it does, in the context of a social network.
—MARK GRANOVETTER

Finding a good apartment in Boston is not easy, especially on the salary of a grad student. In 2005 I had no choice but to learn that lesson.

In 2004 I moved to the United States to join László Barabási's lab at the University of Notre Dame. László, as he is known among those who have spent some time with him, was a renowned young physicist working on networks and complex systems. Before 2004, I had followed László's publications through the Web. Now the time had come for me to follow László himself as he moved to Boston.

In 2005 László was moving his lab to Boston to work a sabbatical at Marc Vidal's Center for Cancer Systems Biology. My first trip to Boston, however, did not involve any research; the only goal was to find a place to live. I had only two days to accomplish that goal.

For two days I rushed from one small, dirty, and expensive apartment to another. Since I had to make a decision quickly, I opted for an apartment on South Huntington Avenue, a short walk from Marc's lab.

At that time I did not know it, but I was going to spend a substantial part of my life in Boston (or more precisely Cambridge, Boston's "secret weapon"). I have now been living in Boston for nearly a decade, and in the meantime I graduated from László's lab, started my lab at MIT, got married, fathered my daughter, and made a lively group of friends. Throughout the years I also lived in many apartments and got to know the homes of many of my friends. So with the wisdom of hindsight I can look back at my first apartment-hunting experience and understand why it is so difficult to find a good apartment in Boston. The reason is simple: the best apartments never hit the market but are passed on informally from friend to friend.

Boston and Cambridge are cities where many people do not stay for too long. Many people here are grad students and postdocs, which means that by definition their positions have an expiration date. Boston and Cambridge are melting pots, but also cities where you make new friends at farewell parties. The combination of high resident turnover and friendships produces a situation in which the best apartments in Cambridge never reach the market. When someone moves out of a good apartment, there's always a friend looking to move in, and landlords usually are okay with this hand-me-down dynamic because it saves them the hassle of finding a new tenant. So the lesson is that, at least in the case of Boston and Cambridge, the real estate market for apartments is secondary to the social network. Borrowing lingo from Mark Granovetter, a sociologist who has studied the economic relevance of social networks throughout much of his life, we can say that in Cambridge the market for student apartments is *embedded* in the network of social interactions.

During the last chapter I focused extensively on the ability of networks to accumulate knowledge and knowhow, but I did not stop to consider the effect of social and cultural forces on the size, structure, and adaptability of these networks. Yet, as the apartment-hunting example illustrates, an understanding of human networks based solely on economic considerations is incomplete. In fact, our interactions, even those that are professional, are constrained by whom we know and by the slow dynamics of relationship building. The purpose of this chapter is to incorporate these considerations explicitly by looking at the basics of social and professional network formation and at the effect of social and cultural forces, such as trust and the family, on the size, adaptability, and composition of social and professional networks.

Describing the literature at the intersection of social networks and economics is not an easy task, in part because this is an area in which differences of opinion are not rare. Economists and sociologists often wind up at the opposite ends of this debate. For much of the twentieth century, economists—particularly those in the neoclassical tradition—treated social structure as an epiphenomenon of market forces. Markets provided incentives for people to connect, and therefore people created and destroyed links fluidly in response to these incentives. This view of the world, which was honed primarily by the use of mathematical models, did not sit well with sociologists and political scientists, nor with their data. In the second half of the twentieth century sociologists and political scientists began pushing back, giving rise to the field of economic sociology and to the theory of social capital.[1]

Economic sociologists argued that social networks had a role to play in our understanding of the economy because social networks often predate economic links, and also because they are strong enough to drive economic outcomes.[2] Not surprisingly, a chief battleground of the debate was the study of labor markets. Labor markets are a fundamental point of intersection between social networks and economic activity, since they can be understood both as the mechanisms by which people grow the networks we call firms and as the mechanisms by which people find networks where they can contribute their work. The view of labor markets that twentieth-century economists grew accustomed to, however, was one in which preexisting social networks did not play a role. Instead, labor allocation was assumed to be the result of supply and demand forces that drove labor markets to equilibrium as wages communicated information about the excess supply and demand of the skills needed by each firm and those embodied in each worker.

Yet the data produced by sociologists such as Mark Granovetter were not kind to these theories. As Granovetter noted in his 1974 book *Getting a Job*, "Perfect labor markets exist only in textbooks."[3]

A landmark study was Granovetter's PhD thesis, which was built on an unprecedented survey of the job searching behavior of professional, technical, and managerial workers in the Boston suburb of Newton. Granovetter observed that preexisting social networks, rather than market forces, were the primary means by which people found jobs. Almost 56 percent of his sample, he noted, had found their latest job through personal contacts, which he defined as contacts established not with the purpose of finding a job, and that involved mostly friends and family.

Yet Granovetter found that social networks not only drove the allocation of workers into jobs but also predicted important characteristics of the jobs these workers obtained. For instance, he found that people who got their jobs through personal contacts had better-paying jobs than those who got them through direct applications or professional recruiting agencies. Also, people who found their jobs through personal contacts were more likely to have a new job cut out for them and they reported higher levels of job satisfaction.[4] In short, he found not only that social networks were the main determinant of information about job availability, which is crucial for job seekers, but also that these networks were correlated with important job characteristics such as wages and job satisfaction. The allocation of the best jobs, just like that of the best apartments, tends to piggyback social networks.

Granovetter's findings, which applied to white-collar workers, showed that personal contacts were the main way these workers found jobs. But by comparing his data with other sources, he also found that this was not different from the way in which blue-collar workers found jobs. With a few exceptions, subsequent studies in and outside the United States have confirmed that personal contacts are crucial for people to find job opportunities. The Panel Study of Income Dynamics, which followed five thousand American families in which the household heads and their spouses were under age forty-five, found in 1978 that 52 percent of white men, 47.1 percent of white women, 58.5 percent of black men, and 43 percent of black women found their current job through friends and relatives. The National Bureau of Economic Research's 1989 Study of Disadvantaged Youths found that 51 percent of whites and 42 percent of African Americans in three poor neighborhoods of Boston found jobs through personal contacts. In Japan the 1982 employment survey showed that 34.7 percent of those older than fifteen found jobs through contacts; other studies gave figures as high as 70 percent for particular cities. Also the effects of social networks have not waned with time. A recent article in the *New York Times* reported that 45 percent of non-entry-level placements in the accounting firm Ernst & Young were employee recommendations, while Deloitte got 49 percent of its experienced hires from referrals.[5] In both cases the numbers are up since the 2008 crisis, as the tightening of the labor market has enhanced the importance of social networks in finding a job. All in all, the evidence appears to show that social networks help drive the formation of professional networks, making questions of social network formation of crucial relevance for the economy.[6]

The economic importance of social networks drives us to ask the following question: How are social networks formed? The basics of social network formation is based on three simple ideas: shared social foci, triadic closure, and homophily. The first two ideas help us understand where we get our friends. A shared social foci means simply that links are more likely to form among people who share a social focus (i.e., classmates, workmates, people who attend the same church, etc.), whereas triadic closure means that links are more likely to form among people who share friends. Homophily, on the other hand, attempts to explain the links that stick—it is the idea that links are more likely to form among people who have similar interests and characteristics. An outcome of these tie formation mechanisms is that social networks are composed of clusters of similar people, who often have highly overlapping knowledge and information. This redundancy is important for the studies on job searches described above, since they tell us that social networks will tend to bring into a firm people who are similar to the ones already there. This similarity is both positive and negative, since it can more easily introduce someone who would be a good social and professional fit with other members of the firm, but it can also increase the redundancy of the knowledge accumulated in the firm to unhealthy levels, or it can represent an implicit form of discrimination (as social networks also tend to be racially and ideologically segregated).

Social networks provide the underlying "grid" that constrains the formation of professional networks. That's one of the reasons Granovetter talks about the economy as a system being *embedded* in social networks.[7] Yet social networks and social institutions do not only affect networks by driving the labor market. In fact, social institutions, such as the family and a society's level of trust, also play an important role in the formation of professional networks, affecting the size and composition of firms in an economy.

Francis Fukuyama is a political scientist who has explored the intersection of culture, governments, and markets deeply throughout his career. In his 1995 book *Trust*, he argues that the ability of a society to form large networks is largely a reflection of that society's level of trust. Fukuyama makes a strong distinction between what he calls "familial" societies, like those of southern Europe and Latin America, and "high-trust" societies, like those of Germany, the United States, and Japan. Familial societies are societies where people don't trust strangers but do trust deeply the individuals in their own families (the Italian Mafia being a cartoon example of a familial society). In familial societies family networks are the dominant form of social organization where economic activity is embedded, and are therefore societies where businesses are more likely to be ventures among relatives. By contrast, in high-trust societies people don't have a strong preference for trusting their kin and are more likely to develop firms that are professionally run.

Familial societies and high-trust societies differ not only in the composition of the networks they form—as in kin and non-kin— but also in the size of the networks they can form. This is because the professionally run businesses that evolve in high-trust societies are more likely to result in networks of all sizes, including large ones. In contrast, familial societies are characterized by a large number of small businesses and a few dominant families controlling a few large conglomerates.

Yet, as we have argued before, the size of networks matters, since it helps determine the economic activities that take place in a location. Larger networks are needed to produce products of higher complexity and, in turn, for societies to achieve higher levels of prosperity. So according to Fukuyama, the presence of industries of different sizes indicates the presence of trust. In his own words: "Industrial structure tells an intriguing story about a country's culture. Societies that have very strong families but relatively weak bonds of trust among people unrelated to one another will tend to be dominated by small, family-owned and managed business. On the other hand, countries that have vigorous private nonprofit organizations like schools, hospitals, churches, and charities, are also likely to develop strong private economic institutions that go beyond the family."[8]

Viewing the industrial structure of a country as an expression of knowledge or as an expression of trust is not contradictory. Large networks can accumulate more personbytes of productive knowledge, and the societies having the trust that favors the proliferation of large networks, such as Japan, the United States, and Germany, will gravitate toward activities that require large networks, such as the production of pharmaceuticals and aircraft. Yet just as a wineglass is agnostic about the type of wine that fills it, the trust that enables the emergence of these large networks does not determine whether these networks accumulate knowledge on auto manufacturing or jet engine production. In other words, the mechanisms that give rise to the network and those that are responsible for the network's contents are different. Trust, which is an essential form of social capital, is the "glue" needed to form and maintain large networks. It is different from the knowledge and knowhow that we accumulate in these networks.[9] Ultimately, this makes the knowledge and knowhow accumulated in networks a different factor of production than the trust, or social capital, that enables the formation of the networks where this knowledge is accumulated.

But how does trust enable the formation of large human networks? Isn't trust a consequence of these networks rather than its cause? Certainly the recurring social interactions that take place at work and in civil associations can reinforce trust. People become friends with their coworkers. Yet there are also good reasons to believe that social networks predate modern economic activity. In a recent study of the social networks of the Hadza, a population of hunter-gatherers in Tanzania, researchers found important structural similarities between the social networks formed by the Hadza and those found in industrialized societies.[10] Moreover, the researchers found that cooperating individuals were more likely to have links with other cooperating individuals, suggesting that social institutions appear to be embodied in social clusters even for the Hadza.[11] As the team of researchers puts it, "Certain elements of social network structure may have been present in an early point in human history"—a point that, of course, might be much earlier than the emergence of modern markets.

It is important to remark that the preexisting nature of social ties does not invalidate Coase's arguments on the cost of links. On the contrary, transaction cost theory and economic sociology are complementary, since the economic effects of preexisting social networks can be interpreted in terms of the cost of links. In the words of Fukuyama: "Certain societies can save substantially on transaction costs because economic agents trust one another in their interactions and therefore can be more efficient than low trust societies, which require detailed contracts and enforcement mechanisms."[12] James Coleman, a sociologist well known for his work on social capital, has also emphasized the ability of trust to reduce transaction costs. In his seminal paper on social capital Coleman described the transactions between Jewish diamond merchants in New York, who have the tradition of letting other merchants inspect their diamonds in private before executing a transaction. He argues that trust and the social network of family and acquaintances that implicitly enforces this trust are essential to make these interactions feasible. In the absence of trust these simple interactions would quickly become expensive, as they would require costly and time-consuming contracts, insurance, and enforcement procedures.[13]

So trust and the social networks that it enables offer an alternative to the formal institutions described by Oliver Williamson. Trust provides a noncontractual, informal, yet highly efficient mechanism to deter malfeasance and enable otherwise risky commercial interactions. In fact, when available, trust is a more efficient channel for the formation of economic networks than formal institutions are, since it works without the burden of costly paperwork and enforcement procedures. By making links cheaper, trust enables the formation of larger networks that can accumulate more personbytes of knowledge.

Social institutions, such as the relative importance of family and a society's level of trust, can help us understand differences in the size of the networks that people form, and hence in the economic activities present in a location. This is true in an international context, but it also works within countries, which often are not culturally homogeneous.

A famous example of within-country variation in social institutions, with consequences for the performance of economic networks, is represented by the contrast between Silicon Valley and Boston's Route 128. Route 128 was a technology cluster that competed with Silicon Valley until it began to wane in the 1980s. According to AnnaLee Saxenian, a regional economic development expert who has written extensively on these two clusters, social institutions are among the factors that help explain the difference between these two clusters:

> [Silicon Valley's] dense social networks and open labor markets encourage entrepreneurship and experimentation. Companies compete intensely while at the same time learning from one another about changing markets and

technologies through informal communication and collaborative practices. Loosely linked team structures encourage horizontal communication among firm's divisions and with outside suppliers and customers. The functional boundaries within firms are porous in the network-based system, as are the boundaries among firms and between firms and local institutions, such as trade associations and universities.

In contrast, the Route 128 region is dominated by autarkic corporations that internalize a wide range of productive activities. Practices of secrecy and corporate loyalty govern relations between these firms and their customers, suppliers, and competitors, reinforcing a regional culture that encourages stability and self-reliance. Corporate hierarchies ensure that authority remains centralized, and information tends to flow vertically. Social and technical networks are largely internal to the firm, and the boundaries among firms and between firms and local institutions remain far more distinct in this independent, firm-based system.[14]

Saxenian's observation tells us how regional differences in social institutions affect the size and adaptability of the networks of firms we know as regional clusters. The firms of Route 128, through their distrust of their employees and other firms, promoted structures that were more hierarchical and less porous, giving rise to a regional cluster that was less adaptable. This lack of adaptability, in turn, translated into a difference in size, since over the long run the less adaptable Route 128 cluster shrank with respect to Silicon Valley. So social institutions affect not only the size of the networks that people form but also their adaptability, and this helped Silicon Valley leave Route 128 in the dust.[15]

Silicon Valley's porous boundaries and adaptability are exemplified in Steve Jobs' famous visit to Xerox's Palo Alto Research Center (Xerox PARC) in late 1979. It was there that Jobs learned about graphical user interfaces (GUIs) and object-oriented programming. Ultimately Apple, not Xerox, was the company that succeeded in commercializing these technologies. Intellectual property purists might complain about Apple and not Xerox profiting from these ideas, but a more pragmatic view holds that it was better for the long-term sustainability of Silicon Valley to have Apple (or anyone, for that matter) develop and commercialize ideas that otherwise could have died in the inboxes of Xerox's managers or, worse, might have been commercialized by a company in a competing cluster. Over the long run, these porous boundaries provided the Silicon Valley network with an adaptability that allowed firms to pass the baton to one another, even if that passing of the baton was occasionally unwillingly.[16] This was an adaptability that the Route 128 network lacked and which affected its relative ability to sustain a large network capable of accumulating the personbytes of knowledge it needed to compete with Silicon Valley.

Steve Jobs was able to wander around Xerox PARC because those who brought him there trusted him. Once again, this shows that trust encourages the formation of the large networks that our society needs to accumulate knowledge and knowhow, even if trust sometimes works in mysterious ways. Trust contributes to network size by reducing the cost of links, but also by providing porous boundaries that allow these networks to adapt to changes in markets and technologies. In a high-trust environment links are easier to create, since by definition people in a high-trust environment assume that new links are not that risky. In a low-trust environment, however, people are reluctant to create links with strangers and have to find other ways to form networks.

Trust enables networks, but networks also enable trust. Even in high-trust societies people are not simply gullible and ready to trust any stranger. Social networks help discriminate among strangers by separating complete strangers from those with whom we share mutual friends or acquaintances. That's what makes a

house party different from a bar. In a house party people know
that they must have friends in common. In a bar, that may not be
the case. Going back to the labor market example, we can now explain why employers are keen on hiring referrals. Employers prefer
people who are referred to them by acquaintances and employees
because it is easier to trust someone with whom you share a friend
or acquaintance than it is to trust a complete stranger. Also, people
who are referred are less likely to quit.[17] In general, trust is more
likely to emerge when links are embedded in dense social clusters,
and high-trust societies have been successful at creating instances
that can help catalyze the formation of these dense networks. As
the political scientist Robert Putnam describes in *Bowling Alone*,
the formation of associations among non-kin—in groups such as
Rotary Clubs, the Freemasons, the Boy Scouts, or the Red Cross—
have been historically powerful means to form the networks where
our society accumulates the trust and access to information we
know as social capital. In the United States most of these associations were formed in the late nineteenth or early twentieth century, and at their peak—between 1900 and 1910—they counted as
members as many as one out of every two hundred Americans.[18]

Low-trust societies are less successful at creating associations
among strangers and hence rely more strongly on family links.
Family links have some important properties that make them
desirable in a low-trust society. They predate commercial interactions, they are highly stable, and they are enforced by family
members, who are often willing to help patch things up when
family members begin a feud. Moreover, they are characterized
by a high degree of altruism, they are often expected to be almost
unconditional, and they are sustained not by commercial purposes
but by emotions such as love, friendship, and loyalty. This makes
families islands of trust in low-trust societies but also helps make
family relationships meaningful. As Fukuyama says, "One could
hardly imagine a meaningful family life if families were essentially

contracts between rational, self-interested individuals." The trust that is available in the family hinges on the almost unconditional expectation that family ties will be sustained, providing a network formation mechanism that predates modern economic activity and is therefore different from the network formation mechanisms promoted by markets and formal institutions.[19]

Yet low-trust familial societies face a predicament, since relying solely on family enterprises will not get them too far. Even when family firms can scale to a considerable size, there is still a need for networks larger than those that can be managed by a group of family members. It is here that the duality of low-trust societies emerges, since low-trust familial societies are more likely than high-trust societies to expect the state to catalyze the formation of the large economic networks they lack. As Robert Putnam observes when discussing the social institutions of the familial society of southern Italy, there "almost everyone agrees [that laws] are made to be broken, but fearing others' lawlessness, everyone demands sterner discipline" from the "bosses and politicians."[20]

But familial societies are not restricted to Italy, as Mafia movies would push us to believe. Much of southern Europe, eastern Europe, and Latin America are characterized by familial societies. Even France, despite its history of mathematical rationality, appears to fit the bill, for in France the state has played a pivotal role in the formation of industry, as is expected for familial societies. The French state, for instance, has been heavily involved in large industrial successes, such as the aerospace industry that culminated in the emergence of Airbus and the once popular Concorde. The French state, however, has also been involved in colossal failures, like that of the now forgotten French computer industry. As Fukuyama describes, "The [French] government's Plan calcul of the late 1960s predicted that computing power would be concentrated in just a few mammoth time-sharing mainframe computers, and on the eve of the microcomputer revolution it subsidized development in this direction. The French computer industry, nationalized and heavily subsidized in the 1980s, began to hemorrhage money almost immediately, increasing the government's budget deficit and depressing the franc."[21] The French computer industry is just one of the many examples illustrating that "cultures in which the primary avenue toward sociability is family and kinship have a great deal of trouble creating large, durable economic organizations, and therefore look to the state to initiate and support them."[22]

*   *   *

We began this chapter by asking how social networks and social institutions affect the size, adaptability, and composition of the networks that humans need to form to accumulate knowledge and knowhow. After our short review of the literature in economic sociology and social capital, we can confidently say that social networks and social institutions help determine the size, adaptability, and composition of the networks humans need to accumulate knowledge and knowhow. First, when it comes to size, we saw that the ability of societies to grow large networks is connected to the level of trust of the underlying society. This is consistent with transaction cost theory, since it implies that trust makes links cheaper, allowing networks to grow larger. In high-trust societies, people are more likely to form large social networks through mechanisms of spontaneous sociability. In the past these included the formation of civil associations, but more recently this form of associations has moved to the Web.[23] Low-trust societies, on the other hand, have traditionally relied on family networks, and are more likely to ask the state to develop efforts requiring large-scale sociability.

Second, when it comes to the composition of networks, we saw that social institutions and preexisting social networks affect the composition of the professional networks we form in two important ways. On the one hand, a society's level of trust determines whether networks are more likely to piggyback on family relations. On the other hand, we showed that people find work through personal contacts, and firms tend to hire individuals who trace the social networks of their employees.

Finally, social networks and institutions are also known to affect the adaptability of firms and networks of firms. As we saw in the comparison between Silicon Valley and Route 128, low-trust regions produce networks with less porous boundaries that limit their long-term adaptability. This is particularly important in innovative sectors. Moreover, we also saw that the use of personal contacts for job recruitment acts as a force that can increase redundancy, although it is beneficial for the trust and cohesion of the networks we form.

Of course, you should take these lessons about trust with a truckload salt. It would be wrong to conclude from the preceding discussion that everyone from a developed country is trusting or trustworthy. By the same token, it would be wrong to conclude that everyone from a developing country is not trusting or not worthy of trust as well. Just as I explained before when I said that it was wrong to assume that all Austrians were musically talented because Mozart was Austrian, it would be wrong to assume that everyone from a developed country is trustworthy because developed countries have—on average—higher levels of trust. In most cases, variations between individuals are larger than variations between groups of individuals. Feeling trustworthy, or untrustworthy, because you are from a developed or developing country would be a wrong interpretation of the previous discussion and should be avoided. At the individual level, people need to focus on a person's actions, as individual actions speak louder than categories and words.

*   *   *

This brings us to the end of Part III. In the next chapters, we will move to the implications of a world characterized by fragmented networks that are limited in their ability to accumulate knowhow and knowledge. This will help us understand the empirical patterns of industrial development that can be observed in international trade data and domestic data, and it will also help us connect these industrial structures to economic growth.

Ultimately, information continues to grow in our society as we develop the ability to produce new products, which are packets of information. To produce these products, however, we need to accumulate knowledge and knowhow in networks of individuals. The previous three chapters taught us why we need to subdivide knowledge and knowhow (the personbyte theory), and they also described the economic and social constraints that limit our ability to form the networks where we accumulate that knowledge and knowhow. As we will see in Part IV, the economic, social, and individual constraints that limit our ability to accumulate knowledge and knowhow are what limit our ability to create products, and eventually, they are what explains international differences in economic development. The more prosperous countries are those that are better at making information grow.

PART IV

The Complexity of the Economy

Without knowledge and knowhow our species would be hard-pressed to make information grow. Knowledge and knowhow inform what we do and how we do it. They are the software that powers the social computer that manufactures our cities and objects. But as a peculiar form of software, knowledge and knowhow are trapped in the hardware that runs them. As we have seen, this hardware involves people augmented by machines, and of course networks of people. Yet while our bodies and social organizations bless us with the ability to accumulate knowledge and knowhow, they also contribute to the uneven distribution of knowledge and knowhow throughout the world. Knowledge and knowhow are geographically circumscribed, and this circumscription contributes to international differences in the ability of countries to make. Differences in the ability of countries to make, however, also explain differences in the capacity of countries to buy. So to understand the global puzzle of income inequality and differences in consumption, we need to first understand the global mechanisms that limit the diffusion of knowledge and knowhow. The diffusion of knowledge and knowhow explains differences in the ability of countries to make products, which are essentially differences in the ability of countries to make information grow.

9

The Evolution of Economic Complexity

Why are knowledge and knowhow geographically circumscribed? So far, we have learned that knowledge and knowhow are difficult to accumulate because learning is social and experiential, and the amount of knowledge and knowhow that each individual—and firm—can hold is limited. The limited capacity of firms and individuals to accumulate knowledge and knowhow requires us to chop up knowledge and knowhow and distribute it in networks of firms and people—which, as we have seen, are hard to form. To hold large volumes of knowledge and knowhow, therefore, we need large networks of people. Yet the relationship between the size of a network and the volume of knowledge and knowhow that it can hold not only makes the accumulation of knowledge and knowhow difficult but also implies that moving or copying the knowledge and knowhow embodied in a large productive network is harder than moving or copying the knowledge and knowhow embodied in a smaller productive network.

Studying the geographical distribution of knowledge and knowhow is difficult, however, because knowledge and knowhow are hard to "see." So to study the distribution and diffusion of knowledge and knowhow, we need to find expressions of them that give us indirect information about the locations where these are present. One option is to look at the geographic distribution of industries, since industries can be understood as the expression of the knowledge and knowhow that are embodied in the networks of people and firms that are present in a location. Looking at industries in lieu of knowledge and knowhow is similar to what biologists do when looking at phenotypes (the physical and functional characteristics of an organism) as expressions of genotypes (the information embodied in an organism's DNA). Genes, in their simplest definition, are the segments of DNA that code for proteins, while phenotypes are the physical and functional characteristics of organisms, such as the color of your hair or your susceptibility to hypertension. What I will try to do in this chapter is similar to what much of genetics is about, yet instead of trying to establish a connection between phenotypes and genes, I will try to find a connection between the knowledge and knowhow available in a location and the industries that are present in them.

Phenotypes and genotypes are a useful analogy because they represent a pair of related entities in which one is more easily observable than the other—phenotypes are easier to observe than genes, and industries are easier to observe than knowledge or knowhow. This duality is useful because it implies that we can measure the most visible quantity as a proxy for the other. For instance, mapping the spatial distribution of the genes that cause a person to be tall is currently quite difficult. In fact, there are many genes associated with height, so identifying, detecting, and quantifying the molecular sequences that can help explain the height differences between LeBron James and Danny DeVito is not that easy.[1] Yet just by looking at LeBron James and Danny DeVito we can easily tell who is more likely to carry the genes that are associated with height, even if we do not know what these genes are.

By the same token, if we are interested in mapping the availability of the knowledge and knowhow required to manufacture jet engines, we can simply look at where jet engine manufacturers and designers locate. In simple terms, we can infer that Los Angeles, and not Quito, is oozing the knowledge and knowhow required to make action movies, because every year we observe many popular action movies coming out of Los Angeles and very few, if any, coming out of Quito. So although the presence of industries does not inform us about the specific bundles of knowledge and knowhow required to make movies, it can tell us where the networks holding this knowledge and knowhow are physically located.[2]

Getting good data on the location of industries is not easy, but it is possible. Imperfect expressions of the international connections between industries and locations are embodied in trade data summarizing the products exported and imported by each country; for local economies, such data can be found in government records such as the tax residency of firms, people's contributions to social security funds, and industrial censuses. While most of these data sets are imperfect and limited, they are still among the best we have to map the location of firms and the knowledge and knowhow these firms hold.

These data sets are useful because they provide the empirical counterpart that we can use to test theories explaining the industrial composition of locations. To do so we need to find features of these data sets that are non-obvious (cannot be explained by simple chance), that are shared by a number of different data sets, and that can be predicted from the theories we want to test.

One striking feature that is common to data summarizing the tax residency of firms and data on international trade is a pattern that ecologists know as *nestedness*.[3] What nestedness means should be obvious from the visualizations shown in Box 1. Nestedness is the technical way to refer to the "triangularity" of these matrices. Formally, nestedness is the simultaneous tendency for (1) the least diversified locations—those with a small variety of industries—to possess a subset of the industries present in the most diverse locations and (2) the least common industries to be present almost exclusively in the most diverse locations.

To illustrate nestedness, consider the exports of Argentina, Honduras, and the Netherlands. Of the 50 products that Honduras exported in 2008, Argentina exported 25 (50 percent) of them and the Netherlands 48 (96 percent).[4] Of the 227 products that Argentina exported in 2008, the Netherlands exported 213 (94 percent). These overlaps tell us that the exports of Honduras are—statistically speaking—a subset of those of Argentina, and those of Argentina and Honduras are in turn a subset of the exports of the Netherlands. Now, you might say that it is obvious that a diversified location, one with many industries, will contain the industries that are present in less diversified locations. Yet the nestedness observed in the data is statistically greater than what would be expected from differences in population or industrial diversity, so we call these matrices nested, not just because this subset structure is there, but because this subset structure is statistically greater than the one we would expect from such obvious explanations.[5]

The statistical significance of nestedness is a fact about the distribution of industries in space that pushes us to think deeply about the mechanisms that could help account for nestedness. Once again, this is where the personbyte theory becomes useful.

The nestedness of these industry-location matrices tells us that some industries (and hence chunks of knowledge and knowhow) are present almost everywhere, while others are available only in a few places. But what are the industries that are present everywhere? Are these the industries that embody large volumes or small volumes of knowledge and knowhow? To answer this question, let's look at a few examples.

BOX 1
The Nestedness of Industry-Location Matrices

The figures below show two industry-location matrices. Each row represents a location, while each column represents a product or industry. The figure on the left shows the products exported by each country, and the figure on the right shows the tax residency of Chilean firms. Black dots indicate the export of a product by a country or the presence of an industry in a Chilean municipality. In both matrices, locations are sorted in decreasing order of diversity, while products and industries are sorted in decreasing order of ubiquity. The fact that most presences agglomerate in an approximately triangular form in the upper-left corner of the matrix is known as nestedness. The solid line shows the diversity of each location. The diversity of a location is equal to the number of products exported by a country or the number of industries present in a municipality. The diversity line is a simple estimate of the maximum possible nestedness that could be observed in a matrix. If nestedness were perfect, the diversity line would be an almost perfect divider between the black and white areas.

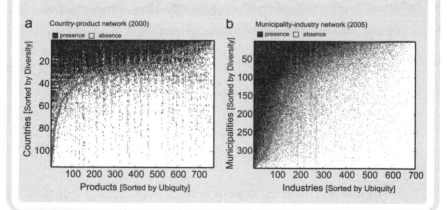

Some of the products exported by most countries include garments, such as underwear, shirts, and pants, while some of the products exported by few countries include optical instruments, aircraft, and medical imaging devices. This quick inspection suggests that "simpler" industries—industries requiring less knowledge and knowhow—are available in more locations. This seems obvious, since making products that require less knowledge and knowhow should be easier. Yet the ubiquity of an industry is hardly a clean measure of the knowledge and knowhow it requires. Among the products exported by few countries we find some mineral resources, such as uranium ore. So the question is how we can distinguish between the rarity of uranium ore and the complexity of medical imaging devices. The answer is that we need to look at the industrial diversity of the countries that export medical imaging devices, which is larger than the industrial diversity of the countries exporting uranium ore.

In general we find that by combining information on the ubiquity of a product and on the industrial diversity of the countries that export it, we can quickly identify products that are more sophisticated than others.[6] The bottom line is that there is a clear trend showing that the most complex products tend to be produced in a few diverse countries, while simpler products tend to be produced in most countries, including those that produce only a handful of products. This is consistent with the idea that industries present everywhere are those that require less knowledge and knowhow. As we will see, these smaller chunks of knowledge and knowhow are the ones more likely to have diffused across the world.

So the first strand in the rope of evidence connecting industrial structures with the availability of knowledge and knowhow is the ability of the personbyte theory to explain the ubiquity of products and the nestedness of industry-location matrices. The personbyte theory implies that the knowledge and knowhow required to make more complex products must be accumulated in larger and more intricate networks, and hence it implies an inverse relationship between the diversity of a location and the ubiquity of the industries that are present in it. Yet, as Robert Putnam suggested cleverly in *Bowling Alone,* a rope of evidence cannot sustain itself by one strand. So the next strands in our rope of evidence will involve using the personbyte theory to explain not only the nestedness of industry-location matrices but also the dynamics of these matrices—that is, the diversification paths of countries and the changes in the geographical distribution of industries.

A useful mental picture that we can use to think about the evolution of a country's industrial profile is a jigsaw puzzle. Indeed, moving a complex industry is like trying to move a jigsaw puzzle from one table to another. The more pieces in the puzzle, the harder it will be to move it, as the puzzle falls apart when we fail to move all of the pieces at the same time. So an easier way to "move" a jigsaw puzzle would be to just move a few pieces to another table where many of the other pieces of the same puzzle are already present and assembled. Attempting to move networks poses the same problems. Products that require more personbytes of knowledge and knowhow represent larger jigsaw puzzles, and hence will be made in few places—since the more pieces you need, the more likely it is that one of these pieces will be missing. Also, the jigsaw puzzle analogy tells us that industries are more likely to succeed in the places that already have many of the pieces that an industry requires. This difference in success rate can be seen as a bias favoring the emergence of an industry in the places, or networks of people, that already have accumulated much of the knowledge and knowhow needed for that industry—because they have developed one or more related industries. In business schools and regional development circles this effect is known as *diversification toward related varieties*, which is technical-speak for the idea that places producing curtains are preadapted to produce tablecloths but not espresso machines.[7]

Similarities in the knowledge and knowhow required by products or embodied in industries can help reinforce the nestedness of the industry-location matrices that we have observed, since they imply that products requiring many personbytes of knowledge and knowhow need the personbytes that are already embodied in the populations of industrially diverse places. Yet nestedness cannot tell us much about which industries are similar, since similarities in the knowledge and knowhow needed to produce pairs of products are poorly reflected in a product's ubiquity. Going back to our biological analogy, we can say that both a zebra and a crocodile might be similar in terms of overall complexity, but evolving a horse from a zebra is easier than evolving a horse from a crocodile, simply because the genes of the zebra already produce many of the features that are needed in a horse (long legs, hair, digestive system optimized for grass, etc.).[8] So to determine if two products are similar, we need measures of similarity that go beyond their ubiquity. Two options here are to use data on the location of industries or data on the occupations that two industries employ. We can use these data to test whether the development of new industries is biased positively toward industries that are similar to the industries already present in a location.

One way to test the predictive strength of industrial similarities is to introduce the idea of the product space: a network connecting similar products. At the global scale, we can construct measures of product similarity by looking at products that are likely to be coexported. This assumes that exporting a pair of products in tandem reveals information about the similarity between them (i.e., if making shirts is similar to making blouses, then countries that export shirts will be more likely to export blouses). For domestic economies where data on the occupations employed by an industry are available, we can connect industries that tend to hire a similar set of occupations (taking these to be proxies for the specific personbytes that the industry requires).[9]

To illustrate the idea of the product space, consider three products: bananas, mangoes, and motorcycles. According to international trade data, we can say that mangoes are similar to bananas and not motorcycles, because the countries that export mangoes have an increased probability of exporting bananas but not motorcycles. According to domestic data, we can say that mangoes are similar to bananas but not motorcycles, because mango-producing firms tend to hire workers in the same categories as banana-producing firms, but motorcycle manufacturers do not.

One neat aspect of the product space is that it lends itself to the creation of beautiful visual representations that can be used to visualize the process of economic diversification. Figure 9 shows a picture of the product space constructed using international trade data. In this network, each node represents a product. Links connect products that are likely to be exported by the same countries. The size of the nodes encodes information on world trade (larger nodes represent larger markets), and node colors separate products in clusters (such as garments, electronics, and inorganic salts). (For a color version of this figure and to explore more than fifty years of international trade data, visit atlas.media.mit.edu.)

The product space is a beautiful picture, but the magic of using it as a representation of the process of economic development happens when you use it to visualize the dynamics of a country's export structure. Figure 10 shows the exports of Malaysia in 1980 and 1990. Here, colored nodes (or dark nodes in a black-and-white display) show the products that were exported by Malaysia, and light gray nodes show the products that were not exported by Malaysia. As a network representation, the product space allows us to

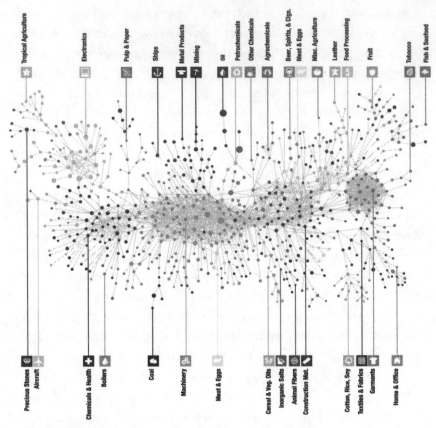

Figure 9. The product space. (Source: atlas.media.mit.edu)

see not only what a country exports but also the products that are related to its exports. In the case of Malaysia we can see clearly that its productive structure evolved toward related industries. In 1980 Malaysia exported a few products in the electronics sector (upper-left cluster) and garments sector (right cluster). By 1990 Malaysia was a more diversified economy, but its diversification was not random. As predicted by the personbyte theory, the diversification of Malaysia went from a set of industries to others that required similar knowledge and knowhow, as estimated by coexport patterns. This is an observation that is statistically true in general and that has been validated by other researchers.[10]

The same observation holds true for domestic data from Brazil, which includes domestic production including both products and services. Here, we use visualizations from DataViva a site I constructed together with Alex Simoes and Dave Landry to visualize data for the entire formal sector economy of Brazil.[11] For illustration purposes we use the Brazilian municipality of Nova Lima. This is a municipality located within the city of Belo Horizonte. Instead of using export data, DataViva uses employment data. This allows us to construct an "industry" space connecting all sectors of the economy, including non-export-related sectors such as education, restaurants, or road construction firms. In the visualization presented in Figure 11, nodes are connected if they tend to hire a similar set of occupations.[12] (For instance, road and railway construction is connected to building construction, since both industries hire civil engineer assistants, construction workers, masonry workers, and excavators, among many other occupations.) The picture that we see for Nova Lima is similar to the one we observed for Malaysia. Yet instead of diversifying in the manufacturing of electronics, Nova Lima diversifies into software publishing and computer consultancy (within the information services cluster shown in the right call-out) and to site preparation, demolition, and utility construction (within the construction activities cluster shown in the left call-out).

Together the nestedness of industry-location networks and the dynamics of countries and locations in the product space represent two important links between the personbyte theory we have discussed so far and the empirics of the world.[13] Since the link between the presence of an industry in a location and the knowledge and knowhow embodied in it is a two-way street, the gradual development of industries indicates that the accumulation of

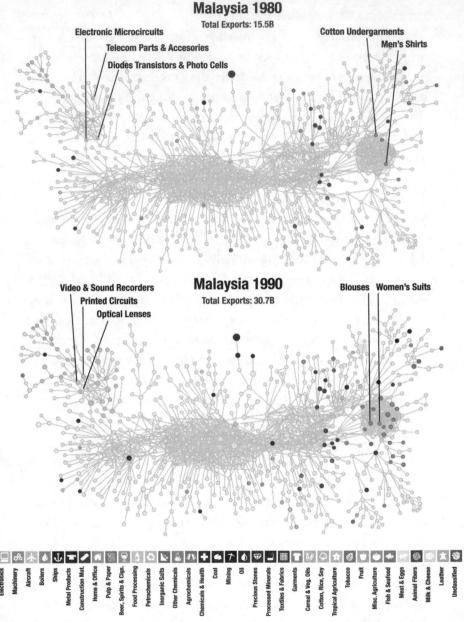

Figure 10. Malaysia in the product space for the years 1980 and 1990. For interactive color versions of this figure visit the Observatory of Economic Complexity (atlas.media.mit.edu) or http://atlas.media.mit.edu/explore/network/sitc/export/mys/all/show/1980/ for the 1980 figure and http://atlas.media.mit.edu/explore/network/sitc/export/mys/all/show/1990/ for the 1990 figure.

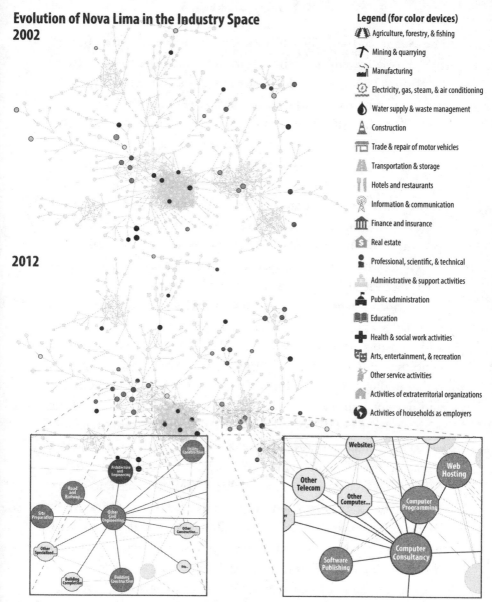

Evolution of Nova Lima in the Industry Space

2002

2012

Legend (for color devices)

- Agriculture, forestry, & fishing
- Mining & quarrying
- Manufacturing
- Electricity, gas, steam, & air conditioning
- Water supply & waste management
- Construction
- Trade & repair of motor vehicles
- Transportation & storage
- Hotels and restaurants
- Information & communication
- Finance and insurance
- Real estate
- Professional, scientific, & technical
- Administrative & support activities
- Public administration
- Education
- Health & social work activities
- Arts, entertainment, & recreation
- Other service activities
- Activities of extraterritorial organizations
- Activities of households as employers

Figure 11. Industry space for Nova Lima in 2002 and 2012. (Source: dataviva.info)

knowledge and knowhow at locations is slow and biased toward the knowledge and knowhow that are already present in those locations. This tells us that knowledge and knowhow need the presence of industries as much as industries need the presence of knowledge and knowhow. In fact, it would be naive to think that the accumulation of knowledge and knowhow is possible in a place lacking the industries that require it. Going back to our gene analogy, we can say that the color of eyes depends on genes as much as the existence of genes for eye color depends on the existence of eyes. So while industries can be seen as expressions of knowledge, knowhow, and other local factors, the opposite is also true: industries represent the structures needed for our species to accumulate these factors, including knowledge and knowhow.

Consider Silicon Valley, a place that packs many personbytes of knowledge and knowhow relevant for making software, hardware, and websites. Silicon Valley's knowledge and knowhow are not contained in a collection of perennially unemployed experts but rather in the experts working in firms that participate in the design and development of software and hardware. In fact, the histories of most firms in Silicon Valley are highly interwoven. Steve Jobs worked at Atari and Steve Wozniak worked at HP before starting Apple. As mentioned previously, Steve Jobs is also famously known for "borrowing" the ideas of a graphical user interface and object-oriented programming from Xerox PARC. If HP, Atari, and Xerox PARC had not been located in the valley, it is likely that the knowledge and knowhow needed to get Apple started would not have been there, either. Hence, industries that require subsets of the knowledge and knowhow needed in other industries represent essential stepping-stones in the process of industrial diversification.

The personbyte theory can also help us explain why large chunks of knowledge and knowhow are hard to accumulate and transfer, and why knowledge and knowhow are organized in the hierarchical pattern that is expressed in the nestedness of the industry-location data. This is because large chunks of knowledge and knowhow need large networks of people to be embodied in, and transferring or duplicating large networks is not as easy as transferring a small group of people. As a result, industry-location networks are nested, and countries move to products that are close by in the product space.

Yet for every rule there is an exception, and on a few occasions productive networks have been transferred. Consider the case of Wernher von Braun, who was brought to the United States after the Second World War to help develop rockets. Von Braun came together with more than a hundred scientists who had worked with him in Germany. Together with his team and many well-prepared US rocket scientists, Von Braun helped that network learn what was needed to advance the construction of space-going rockets. Cases like that of Von Braun's network, however, are hardly the norm in a world where most countries are still unable to manufacture jet engines or space-going rockets. The effort to move Von Braun's network involved an intuitive understanding of the personbyte theory, and historical and political factors also played a role. From the perspective of the personbyte theory, however, we can think of Von Braun's technological transfer as an effort to jump into a new product in the product space. Since in the mid-twentieth century the United States was very well positioned in the aerospace industry, this was an attempt that was more likely to succeed in the United States than in a developing country that was not primed by having many of the pieces that Von Braun needed to complete his jigsaw puzzle.

Now we have two threads of evidence that support the personbyte theory. The first is the ability of the personbyte theory to explain the nestedness of industry-location networks. The second is the ability of the personbyte theory to explain the dynamics of industrial diversification, which is biased toward the production of similar products. The final thread that I will discuss here is a bit different, as it connects the productive structure of countries with income and economic growth. In the next chapter I will show that the mix of products a country exports are highly predictive of its future level of income, indicating that the knowhow that is embodied in a society helps pin down its level of prosperity. Also, by bringing income into consideration I will connect the personbyte theory with traditional macroeconomic models and theories that have been used to explain economic growth. This will help us understand the growth of economies as a consequence of something more fundamental: the growth of information.

10

The Sixth Substance

Hay dos panes. Usted se come dos. Yo Ninguno.
Consumo promedio: un pan por persona.

There are two pieces of bread. You ate two. I ate
none. Average consumption: one bread per capita.
—Nicanor Parra

There are many different ways of describing the economy. One way is to follow the traditional textbooks in macroeconomics and deconstruct the economy into factors of production, such as physical capital, human capital, and labor. Another way is to follow the natural science textbooks and decompose the economy in the same way we decompose everything else: in terms of energy, matter, and information. As we will see in this chapter, these two ways of parsing the world are not incompatible. In fact, knowing how to combine these approaches can be enlightening, since this can help us interpret traditional economic factors in terms of physical quantities and social processes. Also, by connecting economic factors with their physical interpretation we will realize that there *is* one extra factor that we need to consider. That extra factor is the knowhow and knowledge accumulated at the collective level, which gives rise to the diversity and sophistication of economic activities that I call *economic complexity*.

Describing nature in terms of factors of production, such as capital and labor, has a long tradition in economics. Adam Smith decomposed the economy into land, labor, and machinery—the last being a mixture of what modern economists refer to as physical capital and technology.[1] Smith equated machinery, or fixed capital, with an increase in people's ability to produce work, and hence he saw the accumulation of physical capital as a determinant of economic growth. "The intention of fixed capital is to increase the productive powers of labour, or to enable the same number of labourers to perform a much greater quantity of work," he wrote.[2] Smith saw improvements in mechanics, such as those embodied in the steam engine created by his contemporary James Watt, as improvements in the ability of people to produce work: "Improvements in mechanics . . . enable the same number of workmen to perform an equal quantity of work with cheaper and simpler machinery."[3]

During the twentieth century Smith's ideas were mathematized by economists, who used calculus and differential equations to create models of economic growth that hinged on the accumulation of different forms of capital. The earliest models equated economic output to the ratio between an economy's capital and labor when the economy was in equilibrium. They also modeled economic growth as the tug-of-war between an economy's savings rate (the capital that it keeps for later use) and capital depreciation (the wear and tear that erodes capital).

Robert Solow advanced the prototypical model of economic growth in the 1950s—a timely development, as the data needed to evaluate such models were just becoming available. Simon Kuznets, the Russian-born economist who fathered GDP, had finished creating the system of national accounts a couple of decades earlier, helping generate the economic metric that dominated the twentieth century.[4] Solow's model, however, did not measure up well when it was compared with empirical data. As Kuznets famously remarked in his Nobel Prize acceptance speech, "The earlier theory that underlies these measures defined the productive factors in a relatively narrow way, and left the rise in productivity as an unexplained gap, as a measure of our ignorance."[5]

Kuznets' "measure of our ignorance" is what we know technically as total factor productivity (TFP). TFP is how economists refer to the gaps between the economic output predicted by a model and the one observed in the empirical data. (This gap is interpreted as the amount of output that an economy can produce with a given endowment of inputs).[6] This gap motivated economists to build on Solow's work, and during the second half of the twentieth century economists advanced a plethora of new economic growth models that improved the model of Solow.[7] The new models included new factors and new mathematical tools to address the process of factor production and accumulation.

Yet not all economists agreed that the use of aggregation was the best or only path to explain economic growth and development. Wassily Leontief—Solow's PhD advisor and also a Nobel Prize winner—argued that the main problem lay in the reliance on aggregates that disregarded information about specific industries. In his 1971 address to the American Economic Association Leontief wrote, "The time is past when the best that could be done with the large sets of variables was to reduce their number by averaging them out or what is essentially the same, combining them into broad aggregates; now we can manipulate complicated analytical systems without suppressing the identity of their elements."[8] Michael Porter, an influential economist working on competitiveness at Harvard Business School, also had concerns about the overreliance on aggregation. Instead, he advocated for the use of "specialized factors." When discussing the competitiveness of nations in his book *On Competition*, Porter remarked:

According to standard economic theory, factors of production—labor, land, natural resources, capital, infrastructure—will determine the flow of trade. A nation will export
those goods that make most use of the factors with which
it is relatively well endowed. This doctrine, whose origins
date back to Adam Smith and David Ricardo and that is
embedded in classical economics, is at best incomplete and
at worst incorrect. . . . Contrary to conventional wisdom,
simply having a general work force that is high school or
even college educated represents no competitive advantage
in modern international competition. To support competitive advantage a factor must be highly specialized to an industry's particular needs—a scientific institute specialized
in optics, a pool of venture capital to fund software companies. . . . Competitive advantage results from the presence of
world-class institutions that first create specialized factors
and then continually work to upgrade them.[9]

But the mismatch between Solow's model and the empirical
data did not tilt the theoretical scale in Leontief's favor. During
the second half of the twentieth century, economists, with the help
of other social scientists, continued to search for other factors to
incorporate into aggregate models of economic growth.

The first factor to become established in the economic mainstream was human capital—shorthand for the knowledge and
knowhow that is embodied in humans. Human capital was established as an idea by the use of theoretical models, like those
advanced by Paul Romer, but also by empirical breakthroughs.[10]
In an influential paper, Gregory Mankiw, David Romer, and David
Weill extended the empirical comparison between Solow's model
and the available data to include human capital.[11] The measures
of human capital they use consisted of data on school enroll-
ment, a relatively poor proxy for education, learning, knowhow,
or knowledge.[12] Nevertheless, the model accounted for some of

the economic growth that was observed between 1960 and 1985 but was unexplained by Solow's model. The model also confirmed an important prediction of Solow's theory, which was that after taking human capital into account, wealthier countries grew at a more modest rate than less affluent ones. Solow's theory was not wrong, but as is often true of scientific advances, it was incomplete, and the notion of human capital helped complete it.

Yet human capital did not eliminate the gap between data and theory that had been opened by Solow's model—the gap that Kuznets called "a measure of our ignorance." In part this was the result of limitations in the empirical approaches. Schooling is certainly not a great proxy for knowhow and knowledge, since it is by definition a measure of the time spent in an establishment, not of the knowledge embodied in a person's brain. Standardized tests can help incorporate information about a student's basic skills, but they are extremely limited as measures of human capital, since they fail to incorporate information about the diversity of knowledge that is contained in a population of students. Moreover, standardized tests are horrible at measuring important skills such as creativity and conscientiousness. Finally, measures of human capital are also unable to capture information about people's ability to work in teams, since even at the same level of skill some teams can be substantially more productive than others.[13]

So once again the addition of a new factor left an important gap between our understanding of the world and our empirical observations. In fact, the gap was still big enough to motivate the introduction of another form of capital. Starting in the late 1980s, the concept of *social capital* emerged as a powerful explanatory force. Social capital focused not on machines or individual knowledge but on the ability of people to connect.

As we saw earlier, social capital is the idea that social relationships have economic value. This is an idea that makes perfect theoretical sense but is hard to incorporate in empirical estimates. Measuring social capital requires developing measures of social networks and cultural values. Creating these measures is intrinsically harder than measuring stocks of physical capital or even education, especially at a global scale. To measure it, we needed to produce new data.

But social capital is also difficult to measure for another reason: there are many ways for social relationships to have economic value. Consider the distinction between *bridging* social capital and *bonding* social capital, which is a popular distinction in this literature.[14] Bridging social capital, as its name suggests, is the social capital that an individual has when her peers do not know each other. She can arbitrage information or goods between groups that she belongs to, and she can recombine information that is accessible only from her privileged position in a social or professional network.

Bridging social capital is important for selling, brokering, and managing, and has been found to be an important predictor of the success of bank managers and innovative teams.[15] Yet, bridging social capital does not provide a full description of the economic value of human relationships, since the exact opposite to bridging social capital, bonding social capital, is valuable as well.

Bonding social capital is the complement of bridging social capital. Bonding social capital is accumulated in dense social structures characterized by strong links. These are the links we share with our best friends and lifelong collaborators. Bonding links are also the links that we use to produce things, since complex productive activities are not viable among people who do not interact regularly. In other words, bonding social capital represents the tacit ability of a group of people with recurring interactions to act as a team, which is different from the asymmetries of information that allow individuals with bridging social capital to generate economic value.

Bridging and bonding social capital are opposites, but both are important for economic activity. An economy in which everyone is a trader is also an economy where there is nothing to trade. By the same token, an economy formed by tightly knit teams that are rich in knowhow but are not connected will leave plenty of opportunities on the table, since it will fail to produce both, the economic exchanges that it needs to generate to monetize products and the information flows that creative teams need to innovate.

The point is that characterizing social capital is not easy, not simply because of its collective nature but also because once we unpack the idea of social capital we find that it is not simply one thing. The idea of social capital includes bridging and bonding social capital, but also cultural values such as a society's trust in strangers.

These limitations make measures of social capital troublesome to construct, and they also imply that these measures are available only for a restricted number of countries. Yet the trickle of data on social capital that researchers have collected so far still suggests that social capital does contribute to economic growth and also to good governance. In the mid- to late 1990s a number of influential papers began adding social capital to economic growth models, finding a positive association between social capital and economic growth after controlling for the previously known factors.[16] Social capital, even though elusive from an empirical standpoint, was associated with economic growth.

So at the turn of the twenty-first century our understanding of economic growth hinged on five factors: physical capital, human capital, social capital (in which I am also including institutions), land (including geographic factors such as mineral resources, climate, access to an ocean, etc.), and labor (aka people). Certainly we can debate about the size, grouping, and economic relevance of each of these factors, but what is not up for debate is that these five factors have been considered in past attempts to explain economic growth.

Now I will reinterpret these factors in terms of matter, energy, knowhow, knowledge, and information, and connect these factors with the collective accumulation of knowledge, knowhow, and information that I described in the previous chapters.

Consider physical capital. Examples of physical capital include a washing machine, a building, a car, a cement truck, and a spoon. A washing machine is physical capital for a Laundromat, much as a spoon is part of the physical capital of a restaurant. What all of these objects have in common, however, is that they are crystals of imagination. So we can describe physical capital in our language as the physical embodiment of information that carries the practical uses of the knowledge and knowhow used in their creation. Physical capital is made of embodied information and it is equivalent to the crystals of imagination described in detail in Part II.

Now let's turn our gaze to human capital and social capital. Human capital is society's stock of the knowledge and knowhow embodied in individuals. This is different from the knowledge and knowhow embodied in networks of individuals. Social capital, on the other hand, is the ability of a society to connect—the ability of a society to form the networks that are needed to accumulate many personbytes of knowledge and knowhow. Yet social capital is not the knowledge or knowhow embodied in these networks; rather, it is the ability to create these networks, an ability that, as we saw earlier, hinges on personal values, communication and transportation technologies, standards, and trust.

What is missing from this conceptual picture is the knowledge and knowhow that a society accumulates collectively, in firms and networks of firms. As we will see, this contributes greatly to our ability to explain economic output and predict future economic growth.

Before I explain how we can characterize the knowledge and knowhow that a society holds collectively, it is important to discuss a vital distinction. This is the difference between the idea of a *stock*, which is commonly used in aggregate models of economic output and growth, and the idea of *diversity*, which is crucial for

Figure 12.[17]

the creation of models that take into account the identity of the elements in the model.

As I mentioned previously, a shortcoming of traditional measures of human capital, such as years of schooling or scores on standardized tests, is that these measures fail to capture any information about the diversity of knowledge and knowhow that is embodied in a network of individuals (see Figure 12). Some students might be more talented as athletes, while others might have a knack for crafts, math, or languages. Tests, however, fail to capture information about this diversity because they are designed to measure the overlap of knowledge among students, usually by considering a narrow set of skills.

We can make a similar criticism about measures of physical capital. The traditional way of thinking about a stock of physical capital is to add up items in terms of their prices. If we aggregate in this way, we could say that as long as the prices add up to the same total, a kitchen with three stoves but no utensils is equivalent to a kitchen that has just one stove but everything else that we need to prepare a meal. The idea of using market prices to aggregate items assumes implicitly a market where we can trade the items that we do not need for the ones we do.[18] So in the kitchen example, we could trade our extra stoves for the utensils we lack. While this argument works well in theory, in practice it is not always easy to trade capital. Many forms of capital have specialized uses and are sought after by only a few people in the market. Moreover, when we consider infrastructure, we are entering a territory where changing items or projects is virtually impossible. Try trading three bridges that you have for an airport that you don't, or a cellphone network for a highway system. So if we are to honor Leontief's advice and preserve the identity of the elements involved in economies, we need to consider measures that focus on diversity rather than stock, not just when we are thinking about physical capital but also when we are thinking about knowledge and knowhow. By focusing on diversity we adopt descriptions of the economy that do not add apples and oranges, or car mechanics and miners, but which instead can gauge economic capacities while honoring these obvious distinctions.

But how can we create a description of the economy that incorporates the identity of its elements? Once again, we will use data on industries and products. As I argued in the previous chapter, the mix of products exported by a region's industries represents a fingerprint of the region's productive capacities that does not suppress the identity of the economic elements involved. So data on industries and products tell us not only about the knowledge and knowhow embodied in the region's productive networks but also about its diversity of physical and human capital.

To take an example, the production of jet engines tells us about the existence of people skilled in aerodynamics, mechanics, materials, and thermodynamics, and also about the presence of the specialized facilities needed to design, test and manufacture turbines. Now consider the exports of fresh fruit. This tells us about the presence of knowhow in agriculture, and also about the existence of cold-storage facilities supported by a stable source of power. Moreover, exports of fresh fruit tell us about the presence of a customs authority that is efficient enough to dispatch the fruit before it spoils, and also about compliance with international sanitary and phytosanitary standards. So the exports of products can tell us about not only knowhow and knowledge and the diversity of physical capital, but also about the quality of the formal institutions involved.

The idea that products represent a viable way of characterizing economies without suppressing the identity of its elements can be found in Leontief's writings.[19] His work was based on input-output matrices, which summarized the fraction of an industry's output used as other industries' input. Here, however, we will advance Leontief's vision, not by using input-output matrices but by focusing on export data instead. Export data do not have information linking different economic sectors, but it does have the advantage of being available for most countries and a large number of years. Moreover, these data are available at a resolution that is considerably more disaggregate than most of the input-output data that are made publicly available (up to a thousand products, instead of tens of industries). So export data provides us with a lens that has the resolution we need to study economies while preserving the identity of the elements involved.

As we saw earlier, it is possible to characterize a product not just by looking at its ubiquity—the number of countries that export it—but also by looking at the diversity of the countries that export it. Furthermore, we saw that it is important to use both the ubiquity of a product and the diversity of its exporters, as this allowed us to differentiate between products that had low ubiquity because they were rare (such as uranium ore) and products that had low ubiquity because they were complex (such as optical instruments). Now I will use a similar argument to characterize economies.

As a first approximation, we can consider simply the number of different products that an economy makes or exports. Economies that export more products are more likely to embody a larger diversity of knowledge and knowhow at both the individual and collective levels. Yet diversity—measured by counting the number of different products that an economy exports—will not take us very far, since diversity fails to incorporate any information about the complexity of the products exported by an economy. Two economies that export the same number of products are not necessarily equally complex, since one can export products that are simpler than the other's. Once again we need to correct for this limitation. This time we will use ubiquity to incorporate information about the identity of the products exported by an economy. So we can create a more nuanced description of an economy by considering both the diversity of a country and the average ubiquity of the products that it exports.

Considering the ubiquity of the products exported by an economy takes our characterization further, but there are still plenty of shortcomings. As we saw earlier, the ubiquity of a product is a rough proxy for its complexity; hence characterizing an economy by the number of products that it exports and the average ubiquity of these products provides a rough description of an economy. To further refine our measure of that economy, we again need to improve our measure of the products it exports. And, once again, we can use the diversity of the countries that export a product as a way to refine the information contained in that product's ubiquity.

This exercise may seem to be rather circular, as we are using the diversity of countries to improve our measures of products, while also using the ubiquity of products to improve our measure of countries. This circularity, however, has a well-defined mathematical limit. The result of this process is a measure that I developed in 2008 and named *economic complexity*. As we will see, the magic of this measure is that it is highly predictive of future economic growth.[20]

To see how this measure of economic complexity works, let us look at an example. Figure 13a plots the GDP per capita of a country against the country's diversity, measured by the number of products that it exports. Figure 13b is a more complicated version that plots GDP per capita against a measure including the average diversity of the countries that export the products exported by countries that export what an economy exports. This is closer to our measure of economic complexity, and also, a tongue-twister that is at the edge of what we can describe in plain language, but as I will explain, it has some clear advantages over simpler measures of diversity.

In Figures 13a and 13b I have highlighted three countries, Singapore, Chile, and Pakistan. I chose these three because they exported the same number of products in the year 2000, and hence we cannot distinguish among them using only the number of products they export (their diversity). Because Singapore, Chile and Pakistan differ largely in their GDP per capita, but not in the number of products they export, they are aligned vertically in Figure 13a. This alignment vanishes once we start incorporating information about the ubiquity of the products these countries export and the diversity of the countries that export these products. Figure 13b shows Singapore to the right of Chile, and Chile to the right of Pakistan. This shift tells us that incorporating information about the identity of the products that a country exports (via their ubiquity and the diversity of the countries that export them) helps us identify the economy of Singapore as more complex than the economy of Chile, and that of Chile as more complex than that of Pakistan.

Yet, the correlation between this measure of economic complexity and GDP per capita is not what is most surprising. What

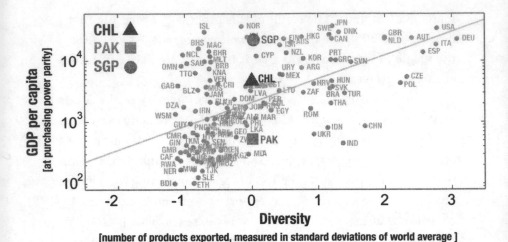

Figure 13a. GDP per capita versus export diversity for year 2000.

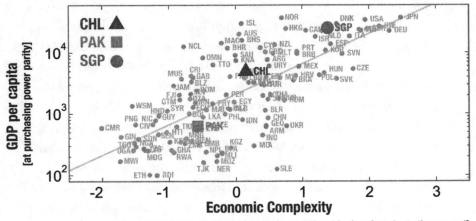

Figure 13b. GDP per capita versus economic complexity for year 2000.

makes this measure of economic complexity important is its ability to explain changes in GDP per capita over long periods of time.

To illustrate the ability of economic complexity to explain economic growth, consider Figure 14. Here we show the complexity of economies (calculated by using the full mathematical formula) and

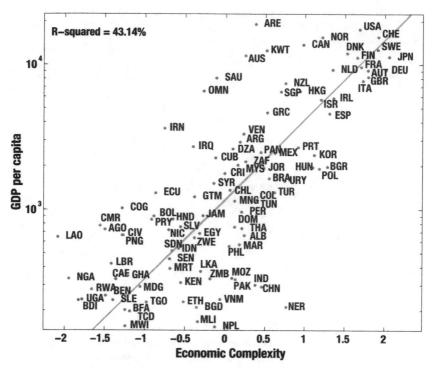

Figure 14. Economic complexity versus GDP per capita in 1985.

GDP per capita for 1985. There are three possible positions that a country can occupy in this chart. Countries that are above the line have a GDP per capita that is higher than what would be expected from the complexity of their economies. Countries that are below the line are countries with a GDP per capita that is lower than what would be expected from the complexity of their economies. Finally, countries on the line are countries with a GDP per capita that is exactly what would be expected based on the complexity of their economy.

So how do these gaps evolve over time? For the most part, countries that are below the line, such as India and China, tend to grow faster than those on the line or above the line (Figure 15). This means that over long periods of time, the income of countries

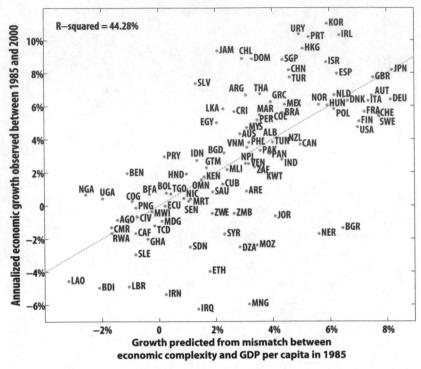

Figure 15. Comparison between the growth predicted from the mismatch between economic complexity and GDP per capita in 1985 and the growth observed between 1985 and 2000.

tends to follow the information that is captured by this measure of economic complexity—in short, countries' incomes are predicted by the complexity of their economies. To earn, you need to make.

But over what time scales is economic complexity predictive of future economic growth? It is interesting to note that economic complexity does not predict economic growth accurately for short time scales, of less than five years. These tend to be dominated by fluctuations caused by periods of crisis, changes in commodity prices, and to some extent variations in exchange rates. Over longer periods of time (ten to fifteen years), economic complexity is highly predictive of future economic growth, meaning that these measures capture information about the capacity of an economy to generate income over the long run.

One way to think about the dynamic between economic growth and economic complexity is that the products a country makes and exports determine its equilibrium level of income. That means that the average income of a country should approach, slowly, the income of other countries with a similar level of economic complexity. Another way to think about this dynamic is that each industry and occupation gravitates toward its own level of income. For instance, skilled software developers are paid well, no matter where they are located, and fruit pickers are paid poorly, no matter where they are picking fruit. This does not mean that the salaries for each occupation and industry are the same across all countries, since they are clearly not; rather, international differences in salaries pull the salaries of those working in the same industries toward a similar value, even if this pull works slowly and is not very strong.[21]

There is plenty more that we can learn from a view of the world in which we juxtapose GDP per capita with the complexity of an economy. One immediate lesson is that low salaries per se do not provide an economic advantage. An economic advantage exists only for those countries that have low salaries relative to the complexity of their economy.

Consider the migration of manufacturing from the United States to China. Over the past decades, the US media have repeatedly used low salaries as an explanation of this shift. Yet there are a number of countries with salaries that are significantly lower than those paid in China and which also have large populations: think of Indonesia, with more than 200 million people; Ethiopia, with 80 million people; and Nigeria, with more than 100 million people. Nigeria and Indonesia have a GDP per capita that is about half that of China, and Ethiopia, is estimated to have one-tenth of the GDP per capita of China. The reason manufacturing has not shifted to these countries is simply that these countries lack China's capacity to make products—a capacity that is embodied in Chinese cities, firms, and people. Informal evidence of this high capacity can be gathered by talking with anyone who manufactures batches of products in a Chinese manufacturing hub, such as Shenzhen. Foreigners who manufacture mobile phones and electronics there will be the first ones to tell you that they chose Shenzhen because this is the best place to build their products. In Shenzhen the personbytes of knowledge needed to manufacture a variety of products are well oiled and ready to go, and firms manufacture there primarily because they want to tap into these capacities, not just because salaries are low.[22]

* * *

We began this chapter by summarizing well-known connections between economic growth and factors of production, from physical capital to human capital, and from human capital to social capital. These factors helped us explain a good amount of the world's variation in economic growth, but we also saw that they are limited by important technical and conceptual weaknesses. One of the weaknesses of aggregate factors is their inability to incorporate information about the identity of the elements that compose an economy. By focusing on measures of stock rather than diversity, these factors added apples and oranges, stoves with refrigerators, and graphic designers with electrical engineers. This limitation was known to be problematic, as Leontief and others warned us about the perils of aggregation. But this was a limitation that was hard to resolve in practice.

By using data on the products exported by each country, however, it is possible to create measures of an economy that conserve the identity of the elements involved. We can do this in part because the data connecting countries to the products they export takes the form of a network. In a network, the identity of an element is expressed not only in internal characteristics (which might define the identity of a product or country intrinsically) but also in the connectivity patterns of a node, which for a country involve its first neighbors (the number of products that it is connected to), its second neighbors (the ubiquity of the products that it makes), its third neighbors (the average number of countries that are connected to the products that a country is connected to), and so forth.

Certainly this is not the only way to measure the complexity of an economy. The same data can be treated in different ways. Also, we can use different data, such as that connecting countries to industries and industries to occupational categories, to create measures that hinge on the structure of the network of locations and occupation instead of industries and locations. The lesson here is not that economic complexity is the only or best measure, but that the complexity of the economy can be measured by developing network techniques that preserve the identity of the economic elements involved.

The payoff of this new measure is high, however, since it provides a predictive metric of aggregate economic output that incorporates not just information about previously explored factors, such as institutions, social capital, and human capital, but also information about the knowledge and knowhow that an economy accumulates collectively.

In the next chapter we will step away from national economies, factors of production, and GDP and take a more narrative, biological, and historical perspective in which we compare the ability of groups of people to pack and unpack knowledge and information with the equivalent mechanisms available in biology. This will help us explore the mechanisms by which systems reproduce their capacity to make information grow.

11

The Marriage of Knowledge, Knowhow, and Information

Until now we have been building a description of the economy based on knowhow, knowledge, their practical uses, and the vehicles needed to accumulate and disseminate both knowledge and knowhow and their practical uses. This is a description of the economy centered on the packing and unpacking of knowhow and information, on how our ability to pack the practical uses of knowledge and knowhow into products augments our capacities, and on how the quantization of knowhow implied by the limited knowhow carrying capacity of firms and people limits its diffusion.

We have noted that information and knowhow are clearly distinct concepts. *Information* refers to the order embodied in codified sequences, such as those found in music or DNA, while *knowledge and knowhow* refer to the ability of a system to process information. Examples of knowhow are found in the biological networks that perform photosynthesis, the process by which plants harvest carbon from the air—or, more fancifully, the human networks that perform "autosynthesis," the process by which groups of humans manufacture cars out of minerals.

Knowhow and information are distinct, but they are also intimately connected. The ability of a system to pack knowhow depends largely on the fluidity with which it can use information
to reconstruct the dynamic networks it needs to accumulate that
knowhow. A seed is a perfect example of this. It is a package containing both the knowhow and the information needed to create
a plant, such as a tree. The development of a tree is nothing other
but the majestic unpacking of knowhow facilitated by genetic information. A seed unpacking into a tree unpacks the knowhow
needed to perform photosynthesis, to build the structures that
will transport nutrients and water from the ground to the leaves,
and to defend itself against pests. A seed unpacking into a tree is
an example of knowhow and information being unpacked into a
structure that is more complex than the one that begot it—the tree
has the ability to perform functions that were absent in the seed.

But how does this unpacking of knowhow and information take
place? Is it the result of information that is packed in DNA, or is it
the result of a more intricate dance involving both the knowhow
embodied in the seed's primordial cell and the information coded
in DNA?

There is a reason trees do not reproduce by simply pooping or
spitting DNA. Such a simple reproductive attempt would not work.
Seeds are much more than genetic material. They contain organelles of diverse kinds without which the information coded in the
molecule of DNA could not be accessed, unpacked, or reproduced.
DNA is essential for the reproduction of biological organisms, but
it is sterile without the networks of proteins and organelles that accompany it in a primordial cell. Throwing a strand of DNA in the
ground is an ineffective way to plant a tree because DNA lacks the
knowhow needed to unpack itself. In fact, DNA has no knowhow
and cannot unpack itself; it is a slave to the machinery needed to
unpack it.

The biological networks that unpack DNA use the templates
codified in the genetic sequence—and the regulatory instructions

implicitly coded in DNA—to manufacture new proteins and organelles on an on-demand basis. These networks construct the structures needed to transform a seed into a tree, showing how the intimate connection between knowhow and information that permeates biology helps biological organisms pack and unpack knowhow with extreme efficiency.

The intimate connection between the information that is coded in DNA and the knowhow that is embodied in a seed's network of biological interactions provides a highly efficient mode of knowhow reproduction and diffusion. Under the right conditions a few seeds can grow into a forest, a queen bee can give rise to a colony, and a few rabbits can take over Australia. Yet the marriage between knowhow and information that permeates biology is lacking in the systems of people and products that we know as the economy.

In both biology and economies larger volumes of knowhow are embodied in increasingly large networks. The knowhow embodied in a rabbit is larger than the knowhow embodied in a fertilized rabbit egg, and it is accrued through the unpacking process known in biology as development. In biology there are also discrete structures that can hold finite volumes of knowhow. Organs know how to perform functions that cells cannot perform, rabbits can perform functions that go beyond those of their individual organs, and ecosystems embody knowhow beyond what is contained in all the members of a single species (for instance, ecosystems know how to regulate environments, even though ecosystems are not conscious of having this ability). These transition points are analogous to the personbyte and firmbyte limits we discussed previously, and they can help us understand the scale at which the marriage between knowhow and information begins to break.

Much of the knowhow embodied in biological organisms can be packed into a tiny vessel containing an information-dense molecule—DNA—and a network with the knowhow required to re-create a complex organism by using the templates and instructions available in that DNA. Yet the knowhow embodied in an ecosystem cannot be packed in such a tight and elegant package. This makes the reproduction of ecosystems much harder than the reproduction of individual organisms, and their decimation much more troublesome. It also makes the analogy between economies and biology more obvious, by highlighting how breaks in the knowhow carrying capacity of networks define the transition points of the system.

At large scales, economies have the reproductive limitations of ecosystems. Economies embody large volumes of knowhow and, much like ecosystems, are only able to embody that knowhow by breaking it up and distributing it in a network of discrete packets—that is, by quantizing it and embodying it in intermediate structures. In economies, firms and people replace herds and organisms, but the quantization principle applies to both. At a finer scale, economies still lack the intimate connection between knowhow and information that is embodied in DNA and which allows biological organisms to pack knowhow so tightly. A book on engineering, art, or music can help develop an engineer, artist, or musician, but it can hardly do so with the elegance, grace, and efficiency with which a giraffe embryo unpacks its DNA to build a giraffe. The ability of economies to pack and unpack knowhow by physically embodying instructions and templates as written information is much more limited than the equivalent ability in biological organisms. These differences imply that in economies, knowhow exists primarily in an "unpacked" form. It is embodied in networks, and although we have some ability to pack some knowhow through "reading" and "writing," our capacity to pack knowhow using information is highly limited. As a result, the knowhow that permeates developed economies cannot be simply transported to other places. Economies do not have the equivalent of seeds, with their intimate marriage between DNA and molecular networks, and so they need to reproduce entire ecosystems to transfer knowhow to other locations. Once again, this explains why know-how is pinned down geographically, and why objects that transfer the practical use of knowhow and knowledge, such as cars, diffuse much more effectively than the knowledge and knowhow needed to make them. So the inability of economies to pack knowhow, because of the lack of an equivalent to the DNA-cell combo, is a fundamental constraint on the spread of economic development, and shows how the packing and unpacking of knowhow represents a fundamental force shaping the structure of the global economy.

As a thought experiment, consider sending a group of ten teen-agers to a desert island equipped with indestructible solar-powered laptops containing full copies of the entire Internet and every book and magazine ever written. Would this "DNA" be enough for this group of teenagers to unpack the information contained in these sources in a matter of five to ten generations? Would they be able to evolve a society that embodies in its networks the knowhow of metallurgy, agriculture, and electronics that we take for granted in our modern society, and which is described in the information that lies dormant in the books and websites they carry with them? Or would they be unable to unpack that information into produc-tive knowhow, failing to re-create a society holding any consid-erable amount of the knowhow that was contained in the society that sent them on this strange quest? Of course, reproducing this "Lord of the Flies" scenario experimentally is unfeasible, but there are examples in our past that tell us that knowhow is often lost when social groups are isolated, and that the knowhow available in some locations is hard to reproduce, even when the attempts to do so are fantastic.

Consider the following three examples. First, we have the sto-ries of the native populations that lost technologies when isolated. As Jared Diamond tells us in *Guns, Germs, and Steel:* "The ex-treme case is that of Aboriginal Tasmanians, who abandoned even bone tools and fishing to become the society with the simplest technology in the modern world. Aboriginal Australians may have adopted and then abandoned bows and arrows. Torres Islanders abandoned canoes, while Gaua Islanders abandoned and then readopted them. Pottery was abandoned throughout Polynesia. Most Polynesians and many Melanesians abandoned the use of bows and arrows in war. Polar Eskimos lost the bow and arrow and the kayak, while Dorset Eskimos lost the bow and arrow, bow drill, and dogs."[1] Certainly these aboriginal groups did not possess the indestructible solar-powered laptops of our previous thought experiment, but also their task did not involve reproducing all of the knowhow of modern society, only that of the society they separated from.

Second, consider the colonies of Jamestown, Virginia, and Plymouth, Massachusetts. The early success of the British colonists who came to what is now the United States was not based on their ability to reproduce European society, but was the result of links with other populations that saved them from extinction. In Jamestown, colonists were literally eating each other before John Rolfe arrived with the tobacco seeds that allowed them to establish a commercial link with England and import all of the things they could not produce but desperately needed. Without this commercial link, the colony of Jamestown would have likely suffered the same fate as Roanoke, an earlier colony that failed to survive. In the United States people celebrate Thanksgiving because Native Americans saved the New England colonists by providing them with the subsistence goods they were unable to produce during the summer. Much like Jamestown, the Plymouth colony required external assistance to survive and a continued umbilical cord with England to begin accumulating much of the knowhow that eventually was transferred to New England.

Finally, I will consider a more modern example. Early in the twentieth century, the Ford Motor Company acquired a large concession of land in the Amazon. This was the size of the state of Connecticut and located on the banks of the Tapajos River.[2]

The "colony" of Fordlandia, as Brazilians called it, was intended to become a large-scale rubber plantation, but it was also a deliberate attempt to develop and engineer a society that, in the eyes of Henry Ford, would be as virtuous as the one he had helped build in the Midwest. But Fordlandia never came to fruition. The inhabitants of Fordlandia did not starve like those of Jamestown and Roanoke, but they shared with them the need to be continuously rescued—in this case by Ford's wealth. The history of Fordlandia is long and disastrous. It includes political and moral battles as well as technical limitations and biological pests. It was also an enterprise that involved the knowhow and experience of skilled engineers and managers who had been successful at the Ford Motor Company. Yet their attempt to re-create the Michigan of the 1920s in the Amazon jungle was not successful. Despite all efforts and several attempts, it was not possible for the mighty Ford Motor Company to transfer the knowhow that was embodied in the networks of people living in the Michigan peninsula to the banks of the Tapajos River.

Hopefully the discussion we have advanced so far illustrates the importance of understanding economic processes through a perspective centered on our ability to pack and unpack knowhow and information, to embody knowhow in networks of people with a finite capacity to carry knowhow, and to create items that embody the practical uses of that knowhow and augment people's abilities.

Yet this is not the last stop of our trip. In the final chapter I will summarize what we have learned about physical, social, and economic systems, and what we have learned about the mechanisms in these systems that contribute to the growth of information.

PART V

Epilogue

12

The Evolution of Physical Order, from Atoms to Economies

The universe is made of energy, matter, and information, and while energy and matter are here by default, information needs to find ways to emerge. This is not always easy.

We began our story by describing some of the basic physical mechanisms that contributed to the growth of information. These included three important concepts: the spontaneous emergence of information in out-of-equilibrium systems (the whirlpool example), the accumulation of information in solids (such as proteins and DNA), and the ability of matter to compute.

The first idea connects information with energy, since information emerges naturally in out-of-equilibrium systems. These are systems of many particles characterized by substantial flows of energy. Energy flows allow matter to self-organize. As Prigogine taught us, the energy flows that keep a system out of equilibrium explain the spontaneous emergence of order or information. Out-of-equilibrium systems beget information naturally as they organize into dynamic steady states. Everyday examples of such systems include the whirlpool that forms when you empty a bathtub or the swirls that emerge when you pour milk into your coffee.

But out-of-equilibrium systems cannot help us understand more complex forms of information. This is where the existence of solids and of the computational capacities of matter comes into play.

The steady march of entropy implies that information is always at risk of being destroyed. To survive, information needs to hide, since a universe where information is short-lived is also a universe where information cannot grow. Solids provide the stubbornness that information needs to fend off the growth of entropy. By allowing information to endure, solids allow information to be recombined. This recombination is essential for the continued growth of information.

In his 1944 book *What Is Life?* Erwin Schrödinger highlighted the importance of solids as information carriers in the context of life. He understood that life was a far-from-equilibrium system rich in its capacity to store and process information. He also understood that solids, such as proteins and DNA, were essential to store and carry information, and that the ability of these molecules to embody information hinged on more than their solidity.

Schrodinger noted that the aperiodic nature of crystalline solids, like DNA, was essential for these molecules to embody information. Long- and short-range correlations allow DNA to pack large amounts of information, just as the short- and long-range correlations of language allow us to express ideas that cannot be embodied in random concoctions of words.

So the second clue in the mystery of the growth of information is that solids are essential for information to endure. Yet not just any solid can carry information. To carry information, solids need to be rich in structure. Random or periodic solids cannot embody the information that more complex structures, such as DNA, can.

The essentialness of solids for the growth of information also tells us about the environmental conditions that are most conducive for the growth of information. A narrow range of temperatures defines these environmental conditions. Information cannot grow in a fully frozen environment, since in such an environment information is static and cannot recombine.[1] Information also cannot grow in an environment that is too hot. In a scalding world, like the sun, far-from-equilibrium whirlpools will be abundant, but the lack of solids means that information has no way to endure, recombine, and grow. There are no long chains of proteins in the sun. In fact, the temperatures are so high that atoms are ripped of their electrons as they dance in the atomic whirlpools of the sun's incessant motion. Hot worlds, therefore, can generate simple forms of information, but without solids, information will be unable to grow beyond its most primitive states.

Energy is needed for information to emerge, and solids are needed for information to endure. But for the growth of information to explode, we need one more ingredient: the ability of matter to compute.

The fact that matter can compute is one of the most amazing facts of the universe. Think about it: if matter could not compute, there would be no life. Bacteria, plants, and you and I are all, technically, computers. Our cells are constantly processing information in ways that we poorly understand. As we saw earlier, the ability of matter to compute is a precondition for life to emerge. It also signifies an important point of departure in our universe's ability to beget information. As matter learns to compute, it becomes selective about the information it accumulates and the structures it replicates. Ultimately, it is the computational capacities of matter that allow information to experience explosive growth.

Out-of-equilibrium systems, solids, and the computational abilities of matter help us understand the growth and presence of information in our universe. These three mechanisms help matter cheat the steady march of entropy, not universally but in well-defined pockets such as a cell, a human, a city, or a planet. But to bring these ideas into our modern reality, we need to recast them in the language of humans, societies, and economies. The growth of information in the economy is still the result of these basic mechanisms. But in these large-scale social and economic systems these mechanisms take new forms.

Our world is populated by structures that are more complex than whirlpools and proteins. These include people and objects. People are the ultimate incarnation of the computational capacities of matter. We embody the capacity to compute, as we organize our brain and our society to beget new forms of information. Objects are where we deposit information. They allow us to communicate messages and coordinate our social and professional activities, but more importantly, they allow us to transmit the practical uses of knowledge and knowhow.

The economy of early hominids and that of twenty-first-century society have enormous differences, but they do share one important feature: in both of these economies, humans accumulate information in objects. Our world is different from that of early hominids only in the way in which atoms are arranged. The objects of today—the arrangements of atoms—are what make our world essentially different from the one in which our ancestors evolved.

The physical embodiment of information is the blood of our society. Objects and messages connect us, allowing us to push the growth of information even further. For tens of thousands of years we have embodied information in solid objects, from arrows and spears to espresso machines and jetliners. More recently, we have learned to embody information in photons transmitted by our cellphones and wireless routers. Yet, what is most amazing about the information that we embody is not the physicality of the encasing but the mental genesis of the information that we encase. Humans do not simply deposit information in our environment, we crystallize imagination.

Our ability to crystallize imagination is the ability to create objects that were born as works of fiction. The airplane, the helicopter, and Hugh Herr's robotic legs were all thoughts before they were constructed. Our ability to crystallize imagination sets us apart from other species, as it allows us to create in the fluidity of our minds and then embody our creations in the rigidity of our planet.

But crystallizing imagination is not easy. Embodying information in matter requires us to push our computational capacities to the limit, often beyond what a single individual could ever achieve. To beget complex forms of information, such as those that populate our modern society, we need to evolve complex forms of computation that involve networks of humans. Our society and economy, therefore, act as a distributed computer that accumulates the knowledge and knowhow needed to produce the information that we crave.

Ultraorthodox interpretations of the economy would argue that this computer self-organizes to an optimal state thanks to the price system. In reality, however, the economic computer is much clunkier than that.

Economies are embedded in social and professional networks that predate and constrain economic activity. These networks are important because they are the only structures that we have available to accumulate large volumes of knowledge and knowhow. Yet, as Granovetter, Putnam, and Fukuyama showed us, the sizes, shapes, and evolution of these networks are constrained by historical and institutional factors, from a society's level of trust to the relative importance we give to family relationships.

So the social and economic problem that we are truly trying to solve is that of embodying knowledge and knowhow in networks of humans. By doing so, we are evolving the computational capacities of our species, and ultimately helping information grow.

So the growth of information in the economy, which is ultimately the essence of economic growth, results from the coevolution of our species' collective computational capacities and the augmentations provided by the crystals of imagination that we are able to make. Crystals of imagination, from airplanes to toothpaste, amplify the practical uses of the knowledge, knowhow, and imagination of our society, augmenting our capacities to create new forms of information. Moreover, these objects allow us to form networks that embody an increasing amount of knowledge and knowhow, helping us increase our capacity to collectively process information.

Our need to form networks, however, emerges from one important consideration: the limited ability of humans to embody knowledge and knowhow. To fight our individual limitations we need to collaborate. We form networks that allow us to embody more knowledge and knowhow, because without them our ability to process information and create crystals of imagination would be highly limited. These networks are essential to produce products that require more knowledge and knowhow than can be embodied in a single individual. To simplify our discussion, we called that maximum individual capacity one personbyte.

The personbyte theory suggests a relationship between the complexity of an economic activity and the size of the social and professional network needed to execute it. Activities that require more personbytes of knowledge and knowhow need to be executed by larger networks. This relationship helps explain the structure and evolution of our planet's industrial structures. The personbyte theory implies that (1) simpler economic activities will be more ubiquitous, (2) that diversified economies will be the only ones capable of executing complex economic activities, (3) that countries will diversify toward related products, and (4) that over the long run a region's level of income will approach the complexity of its economy, which we can approximate by looking at the mix of products produced and exported by a region, since products inform us about the presence of knowledge and knowhow in a region. All of these predictions are empirically testable and are consistent with the available data.

So in the world of atoms and economies the growth of information hinges on the eternal dance between information and computation. This dance is powered by the flow of energy, the existence of solids, and the computational abilities of matter. The flow of energy drives self-organization, but it also fuels the ability of matter to compute. Solids, on the other hand, from proteins to buildings, help order endure. Solids minimize the need for energy to produce order and shield information from the steady march of entropy. Yet the queen of the ball is the emergence of collective forms of computation, which are ubiquitous in our planet. Our cells are networks of proteins, which form organelles and signaling pathways that help them decide when to divide, differentiate, and even die. Our society is also a collective computer, which is augmented by the products we produce to compute new forms of information.

*   *   *

As the universe moves on and entropy continues to increase, our planet continues its rebellious path marked by pockets that are rich in information. Enslaved by the growth of order, we form social relationships, make professional alliances, beget children, and, of course, laugh and cry. But we often lose sight of the beauty of information. We get lost in the urgency of the moment, as our minds race like whirlpools and our lives compute forward in a universe that has no past. We worry about money and taxes instead of owning the responsibility of perpetuating this godless creation: a creation that grew from modest physical principles and which has now been bestowed on us.

ACKNOWLEDGMENTS:
BLEEDING WORDS

The following acknowledgments are inseparable from the series of events that led to this book. As anyone that has bled at the keyboard knows, the art of writing is not just the art of communicating, but also the art of discovering the story you want to tell. That discovery is not easy.

Discovering the book within you is excruciatingly uncomfortable. It involves eating your own mental vomit on a daily basis. You eat, vomit, and reingest half-baked ideas with the hope that this continuous reingesting will help you purify your words. It works sometimes.

Why Information Grows is not the book I sold originally to my agent or publishers, nor is it the book I planned to write in the first place. *Why Information Grows* is the book I discovered in the process of writing another book, a book about economic growth, economic complexity, and development. Through the process of writing I came to realize that economic growth was a shallow topic. Economic growth was a phenomenon that occurred on the social and economic surface of the universe. It was a phenomenon that connected with our irrelevant lives and our anxious urge to

183

feel that our lives are improving (and to our paternalistic need to feel that we are improving the lives of others). But our hedonistic and paternalistic urges are often a poor indicator of abstract depth. If there is something that the humanity of science has taught us, it is that the most relevant aspects of the universe usually hide under the surface. These are truths that go unnoticed but which transcend our shallow human anxieties and our need for more.

As I departed from the problem that had fascinated me for several years and tried to escape the rhetorics of deprivation, guilt, prosperity, optimization, equilibrium, and wealth, I learned that economic growth was nothing more than an epiphenomenon of a larger, more universal, and more relevant phenomenon. This is not the growth that captures headlines and political agendas, but the growth that makes possible the existence of life and society—even if we ignore it. This is the growth of physical order, or information. Soon I had to accept that information was what it was all about. At this point, I could no longer see the economy in terms of income, regulations, and agents. The economy was a mundane manifestation of something deeper. It was the social manifestation of the growth of information, and that was the growth I needed to explore.

The first pages of this book were written on October 2, 2012. I was at Boston's Logan Airport, on my way to Brussels. The plan was to spend one night there, as I was going to present at an event organized by MIT's Industrial Liaison Program. In the anxiety of the overtraveled, overscheduled, and overworked academic life, I began to vomit words into my laptop.

That period was not particularly amenable to writing. Between September and November I visited Tianjin, Beijing, Kyoto, Tokyo, Washington, Brussels, New York, Santiago, and Lisbon. The travel was killing me, draining me of the energy I needed to bleed words. As the year ended I swore not to travel for the entirety of 2013. I wanted to focus on my family and on writing. For the most part, I kept that promise.

During December 2012 and January 2013 I found myself with the time, impatience, and energy that I needed to grow the words I had jotted down into precursors of what are now Chapters 4, 5, and 6. The book grew out of that. The idea that carried these first drafts was the idea of crystallized imagination, which gave the book its working title and also the name of the Dropbox folder where I dutifully saved my words.

The winter of 2013 was also the time when my daughter was conceived and I began to share the wonderful journey of child rearing with my wife, Anna. Anna has always been a great supporter of my life and work, and I am eternally indebted to her.

During this period I also received the support of my dear friend Mridu, who time after time sat next to me while I read her what I had written during the day. Mridu was the main supporter of the book, and I am eternally grateful to her. Without Mridu's continuous support, I would have not completed the book or allowed it to evolve in the way it did.

Getting publishers interested in the book was something that I also needed to accomplish that winter. Selling the rights to a book is a strange process, but I was fortunate to be able to count on the support of Katinka Matson, who helped me hone the book proposal and coached me through the interviews. Katinka connected me with a number of editors, including Tim Bartlett. Tim, who at the time was with Basic Books, believed that the book I was writing could be about more than economic growth. He appeared to understand my madness and was supportive of my work, even as I veered in and out of ideas—and, of course, in and out of writer's depression. Tim helped me improve my writing skills by showing me the importance of adding structural passages to my writing. These are passages in which you tell the reader what you are going to write about, and how it will connect to what you just wrote. Tim was also the editor who gave me the most feedback, revising two full drafts. Unfortunately, he left Basic Books late in 2013.

In 2013 I also developed a writing ritual. Every morning I walked thirty minutes to Voltage, a hipsterish café located close to MIT. Voltage became my main rewriting spot. Every day I would arrive at Voltage sometime between eight and eleven in the morning and would leave at 1 p.m. After bleeding words and battling paragraphs, I would storm out of Voltage, thinking about what I was going to write next. In the evenings, I walked home from MIT often calling my friend Ignacia Echeverria (Nacha). Nacha is a statistical physicist who enjoyed talking about entropy, enthalpy, and information with me.

At Voltage I would always order a Kitsch and the Cactus (a latte with agave syrup as sweetener) and a plain bagel with avocado, which was not on the menu. I also interacted briefly with the baristas, Sarah, Lillian, Anna, Emily, and Lee. For two years our relationship evolved slowly, with a few words exchanged every day. Despite the brevity of our interactions, I drew support from them, and I am also greatly indebted to them for contributing to the environment in which these words took shape. I would be crazy not to thank them.

During the summer of 2013 I wrote what became Chapters 6 and 7 at Voltage. I also studied the ideas of Ronald Coase and Oliver Williamson there. This set the foundation for what became Part III.

In the fall of 2013 this book was still unfinished, but my daughter was ready to see the light of day. Iris' birth changed this book. In a previous draft I already had a narrative explaining birth as an alien process—which had been inspired by Anna's pregnancy—but I was lacking the emotional thrust of the actual event. Iris' birth changed my ability to articulate this idea, and also pushed me to think in new directions.

Iris was born on October 6, 2013, between a Saturday and a Sunday. On the Monday that followed I escaped to the Tip Tap Room, a restaurant I found in Cambridge Street close to Massachusetts

General, and while a bunch of suits ate their lunches, I vomited a new Chapter 1. That first paragraph survived almost untouched by the tens of revisions that came after.

At the time of my daughter's birth I also had been listening repeatedly to James Gleick's wonderful book *The Information*. The book was circling in my car's iPod and motivated me to read the original works of Shannon, Weaver, and Wiener. *The Information* also motivated me to write what is now Chapter 2, although this chapter kept on evolving intensely until the end. I wrote the first draft of that chapter in Café 1369, a coffeehouse located in Inman Square.

The fall of 2013 was the time when I began to work the concept of information into the core of the book. Also, I became increasingly curious about the physical origins of order, but realized that information theory did not explain the physics of information and its origins, since it focused on the mathematics of communication. At a group meeting, I shared my curiosity with my students, and Francisco Humeres, an urban planner who was working in my group, mentioned Ilya Prigogine to me. I was embarrassed about not knowing Prigogine's work, so I rushed to the Web and bought many of his wonderful books. His books helped me understand the arrow of time and the origins of order. I dedicated November to learn about Prigogine's work and wrote what is now Chapter 3.

The original deadline for the book was February 2014, and in December 2013 I was starting to wonder if I could finish discovering my book on time. I also wanted to expand the part of the story describing the origins and structure of social and professional networks. I knew that networks were the fundamental units where our society accumulates knowledge and knowhow, and that the capacity of networks to accumulate knowledge and knowhow was affected by social institutions and sociological process. So I began to dig up literature on social networks and social capital. This was a different network literature than the one that I had learned during my PhD, which focused on the descriptions of networks advanced by physicists.

Olga Avdeyeva, a political scientist at Loyola and a friend of Anna's, suggested Francis Fukuyama's book *Trust*. This was a wonderful suggestion. I spent November and most of that vacationless Christmas break taking care of my daughter and reading Fukuyama, Granovetter, Putnam, and other titans of social capital theory. In January 2014, I put these ideas together in what is now Chapter 8.

By the February deadline I had most of the text that made the book, but I was not 100 percent satisfied with the title, framing, and introduction. Also, I was editorless and, from a writer's perspective, quite lonely. February, March, and April were unproductive times as I focused on teaching, research papers, projects, and other obligations.

In May 2014 I caught a break when Mridu was back in town— she had moved to Seattle late in 2013. We talked extensively about the book while contemplating the Boston skyline from my condo's parking structure. Also, I was finally able to get my new editor at Basic Books, T.J. Kelleher, to answer my emails and connect on the phone. After discussing the book with Mridu and T.J. I rewrote the intro from scratch. It was here that I brought in Ludwig Boltzmann as a key character. Yet in this rewriting I failed to frame the book around the growth of information, instead focusing it on the mechanisms that make it difficult for information to grow. The new introduction framed the book around the quantization of information and computation, which are implied by the need of both information and computation to always be physically embodied. The working title of the book changed from *Crystallized Imagination* to *The Bit and The Atom*.

The summer of 2014 was not easy. I needed to finish the book, but I also needed to complete my case for promotion at MIT and fulfill other obligations that involved plenty of writing and travel.

In August I visited St. Petersburg with Anna and Iris while I tried to complete the book in that city's cafés. I wrote Chapter 9 in two cafés: Candies, a centrally located café near the Hermitage, and Komunalka, a low-key café located close to our apartment on the city's Petrograd side. For the most part, this was a period in which I felt like a pile of dung.

From St. Petersburg I had to go to Colombia, Brazil, and Chile. In that intense trip I got rid of my funk, as daily obligations and good company distracted me from the worries of my unfinished writing. I was also exchanging short messages with Helen Conford, from Penguin UK, as we went back and forth about the book title. The publishers axed *Crystallized Imagination*, which I was still considering, by labeling it as too dreamy.

In Santiago I visited the lab of my friend Carlos Rodriguez, a scholar at the Universidad del Desarrollo. Before meeting with him I also connected with a high school friend, Maria Jose Badinella, whom I had not seen since our high school graduation. After explaining the book to both of them and spending the evening drinking and smoking with Carlos, I made my way back to my parents' home and encountered the phrase "why order grows" circling in my head. It clicked. This was the sentence that I had been searching for during the past two years. It explained the story in a snap. The next day I changed the phrase to "why information grows" and was surprised to learn that these three words were not a common combination (at least based on what Google can find). As of today, November 11, 2014, "why information grows" returns four hits on Google. The first one is the shell of an Amazon profile created for this book by my UK publisher. Two of the other hits are not a complete sentence, since the words are interrupted with punctuation. (By contrast, the phrase "why economies grow" returns more than twenty-six thousand hits.)

If these three words were all I was going to get out of my trip to Chile, I was ready to call the trip a victory. Yet these three words

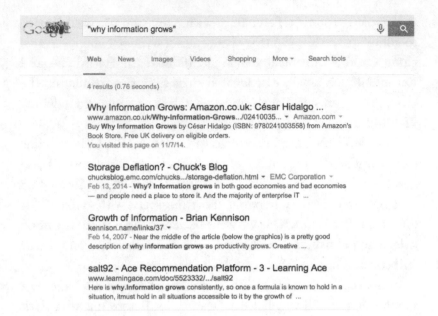

required restructuring the rest of the book completely. Even though I had no time, I was not ready to abandon the book. So I decided to make one final chiropractic maneuver, which involved changing the order of chapters and the connective tissue between them.

I boarded a plane out of Santiago that Saturday, as I had been doing every Saturday for nearly a month, and headed to Leesburg, Virginia. I was scheduled to present at an event organized by the Inter-American Development Bank. On the Sunday prior to the event, in the preppy staleness of a golf club, I started restructuring the book into its current form.

The final restructuring was tough—too tough. After all of that travel I still needed to visit New Haven, New York, London, and Saudi Arabia while I moved my lab into a new building and received four new students in my group. I only had three weeks to put the book in the hands of the editors, and I struggled. During those weeks I woke up in the middle of the night repeatedly, with that feeling of vomit that comes from excess anxiety and the insecurity that commands you to stay up until dawn. The book lost about ten thousand words in that final editing carnage. The support of Anna was essential at this time, as it had been all along.

In these three weeks I also betrayed Voltage and wrote the concluding chapter at Commonwealth, a restaurant close to MIT. Voltage had grown too popular, and Commonwealth was the morning desert I needed to focus on my last words.

I have now abandoned the book. Any bleeder knows that books are never finished, only abandoned. Yet I hope to have reached a point at which the orphan I produced is mature enough to find a home in other people's heads.

Raising this rebellious orphan was not easy and was possible only thanks to the support that I have been lucky enough to receive from those who participated in the production of the book or were kind enough to be my friends. So I would also like to use this opportunity to thank in writing those who are dear to me: Alex Simoes and Dave Landry, who are not only kick as developers and visualization artists but also caring and loving companions; Jennifer Gala, who has always been more of a friend than anyone I have ever known; Dominik Hartmann, Jermain Kaminski, Ali Almossawi, and Ethan Zuckerman, who read tadpoles of this manuscript and were kind enough to share their thoughts with me; my parents, grandparents, and sisters, César E. Hidalgo, Nuria Ramaciotti, Caterina Hidalgo, Nuria Hidalgo, Antonio Ramaciotti, and Nuria Ferre; my students and former students, Shahar Ronen, Daniel Smilkov, and Deepak Jagdish; my Minheiros friends Andre Barrence and Emilia Paiva; and of course, those who betrayed me and turned their back on me in the past.

I am now on the emptiness that comes after an exhausting journey, unsure of whether my words will be ever read. I am not sure if I feel happy, but even if I am not, I appreciate not being unhappy alone. My daughter, Iris, is starting to crawl, stack, and walk; I am seeing her develop her ability to process information, and I am learning about her amazing capacity to love her parents, which I know one day she will forget. Iris and Anna are the biggest sources of strength in my life, and even if they don't actively help me bleed ink on paper, I owe it all to them.

NOTES

Introduction: From Atoms to People to Economies

1. In this context, the word *atom* is used to refer mainly to discrete particles, which could be either atoms or molecules.

2. Two great books describing the interaction between evolution and behavior are Richard Dawkins, *The Selfish Gene* (Oxford: Oxford University Press, 2006), and Steven Pinker, *The Blank Slate: The Modern Denial of Human Nature* (New York: Penguin, 2003).

3. Information theory also has a quantum version, known as quantum information theory. The existence of quantum information theory, however, does not invalidate the claim that classical information is a concept that works at a range of scales that is unusual for other theories.

4. Friedrich Hayek, "The Use of Knowledge in Society," *American Economic Review* 35, no. 4 (1945): 519–530.

5. George A. Akerlof, "The Market for 'Lemons': Quality Uncertainty and the Market Mechanism," *Quarterly Journal of Economics* 84, no. 3 (1970): 488–500.

6. Claude E. Shannon and Warren Weaver, *The Mathematical Theory of Communication* (Urbana: University of Illinois Press, 1963), 8.

7. Ibid., 31.

8. The formula for Boltzmann's entropy (S_B) is $S_B = k_B \ln(W)$ where k_B is Boltzmann's constant, which has units of energy over temperature, and W is the number of microstates corresponding to a given macrostate. Gibbs generalized the formula for entropy by defining it in terms of the probability that a system would be in a microstate (p_i), instead of the

total number of equivalent microstates (W). Gibbs entropy S_G is defined as: $S_G = -\sum_i p_i \ln(p_i)$. Note that Boltzmann and Gibbs' entropies are equivalent $(S_G = S_B)$ when $p_i = 1/N$ for all i, meaning that Gibbs formula reduces to that of Boltzmann's for a system in thermal equilibrium since here all microstates are equally likely.

Shannon's formula for information entropy $H = -\sum_i p_i \log_2(p_i)$, where p_i is the probability that a character will occur. Shannon's formula is functionally equivalent to Gibbs' entropy except for a multiplicative constant. We can use a constant to absorb both, the change in the base of the logarithm (from base 2 to the base of natural logarithms e), and Boltzmann's constant.

CHAPTER 1: THE SECRET TO TIME TRAVEL

1. Another important property differentiating humans from other species is our ability to use fictive language, that is, to use language to invent stories. Interestingly, the evolution of fictive language and complex physical objects is intertwined.

Dating the origins of human language is difficult, since oral expressions largely predate writing. The earliest records of written language date back about eight thousand years, so archeologists wanting to estimate the origins of spoken language need to consult other forms of evidence, such as the complexity of the products found in the archeological record. The idea that complex products can be used to date the origins of human language is based on two lines of argument. First, an individual able to produce a complex tool, such as a spear with a stone tip or a carburetor, understands how different parts fit together, much in the same way that human languages allow us to combine different words into sentences, and sentences into narratives. In other words, individuals who can build complex tools are likely to have an internal way of representing each of the parts involved in the construction of the tool, and can think about the sequences of actions required to put these pieces together. The mental process required to ideate and assemble a complex product can be thought of as a primitive grammar, and it has been found to define similar patterns of brain activity. Making complex products is enabled by a similar combinatorial capacity than the one present in human languages. So even though the combinatorial capacity of product creation does not necessarily imply the use of a human language, it is reasonable to assume that these two combinatorial cognitive capacities emerged together.

The second line of argument supporting the use of complex objects to date the origins of language relates to the diffusion of the knowledge required to make complex objects, such as arrows and spears. The proliferation of arrows and spears can be seen as an indication of the existence of early forms of human language, since learning how to build an arrow is different from learning how to use a rock to crack open a walnut. Simple tasks can be learned easily through observation and imitation, while the production of complex objects involves nuances that are communicated much more effectively among individuals who share a language. For instance, individuals sharing a language can more effectively learn how to safely handle the poison used in making arrowheads, or how to fasten a stone ax to a wooden handle.

Current archeological records show that *Homo sapiens* was fashioning tools as complex as those of some modern hunter-gatherers as far back as 100,000 to 70,000 years ago. This shows that our ability to crystallize imagination largely predates our ability to write about it, and it dates the origins of language and complex products to the time before early humans left Africa. This suggests that it is not the use of simple tools that separated our ancestors from other species but their ability to create complex objects that were superior to those found naturally in the environment. See E. O. Wilson, *The Social Conquest of Earth* (New York: W. W. Norton, 2012), and Yuval Harari, *Sapiens: A Brief History of Humankind* (New York: Random House, 2014).

2. As described by Randall Davis, Howard Shrobe, and Peter Szolovits in "What Is a Knowledge Representation?," *AI Magazine* 14, no. 1 (1993): 17–33: "First, a knowledge representation is most fundamentally a surrogate, a substitute for the thing itself, that is used to enable an entity to determine consequences by thinking rather than acting, that is, by reasoning about the world rather than taking action in it."

3. For those familiar with the literature, I will be building on the distinction between explicit and tacit knowledge advanced half a century ago by Michael Polanyi. I will be using the word *knowhow* to describe tacit knowledge, as I prefer using two distinct nouns to denote two different concepts instead of using the same noun and adding an adjective (*explicit* or *tacit*). For a summary of the concepts of tacit and explicit knowledge I recommend Harry Collins, *Tacit and Explicit Knowledge* (Chicago: University of Chicago Press, 2010). There, Collins divides tacit knowledge into *relational* tacit knowledge, which includes what we could describe in principle but often fail to describe; *somatic* tacit knowledge, which relates to things we can do with our bodies but cannot describe (such as riding a bike); and *collective* tacit knowledge, which involves knowledge that draws meaning from social interactions, such as the rules for language.

4. This quote can be found in the biography of Marvin Minsky on the Computer History Museum's website: www.computerhistory.org/fellowawards/hall/bios/Marvin,Minsky.

CHAPTER 2: THE BODY OF THE MEANINGLESS

1. My friend and undergraduate advisor Francisco Claro suggested this calculation to me a few years ago. His example at that time was a fighter jet.

2. Based on data from goldprice.org, on January 14, 2013, at 16:45 Eastern Standard Time, the exact price was $53,586 per kilo.

3. A good discussion of this can be found in Eric Beinhocker's *The Origin of Wealth* (Boston: Harvard Business School Press, 2005).

4. You might argue that there is much more to the value of a Bugatti than its physical order or information. I agree with you and suggest that you keep on reading. I will be adding these additional considerations gradually.

5. Since *order* is a word that has many different meanings (for example, the arrangement of clothes in your closet, or the food items you request in a restaurant), I would like to clarify the meaning of the word as I will be using it going forward. I use *order* to mean physical order—the way in which the parts of a system are arranged (like the way you want the clothes to be arranged in your closet). By definition, physical order is information. Physical order is what differentiates the Bugatti before the crash from the wreck that was left after the crash.

6. This is the simplest possible case we can use to illustrate Shannon's theory, since it assumes all tweets and characters are equally likely. In reality, all characters and strings of characters are not equally likely. It is much more likely for a tweet to contain the sequence of characters "http://" than the sequence of characters "qwzykq." If Brian knows about these differences, he could exploit them to reduce the number of questions he needs to ask to guess the tweet. If you are uncomfortable with these simplifying assumptions, assume that Abby and Brian come from different planets, and that the only thing that Brian knows about Abby's alphabet is that it is based on thirty-two different characters.

7. Notice that the number 700 is also found in the expression 2^{700}, which is the total number of possible tweets. The general formula in this case is $N \log_2(S)$, where N is the number of characters and S is the size of the alphabet. This is equivalent to $\log_2(SN)$, where SN is the total number of possible tweets. In general, notice that the information content of a message goes as the base-two logarithm of the number of possible messages. This is because the most efficient way to search for a message, or uniquely identify it, is to iteratively cut the search space in half.

8. There are many decision criteria that can eventually lead people to reach those states. For a great introduction to the diversity of behaviors that can result in people occupying the upper half of a stadium or auditorium, read the first chapter of Thomas Schelling's *Micromotives and Macrobehavior* (New York: W. W. Norton, 2006).

9. Manfred Eigen, *From Strange Simplicity to Complex Familiarity: A Treatise on Matter, Information, Life and Thought* (Oxford: Oxford University Press, 2013), 310.

10. Tomas Rokicki et al., "The Diameter of the Rubik's Cube Group Is Twenty," *SIAM Journal on Discrete Mathematics* 27, no. 2 (2013): 1082–1105.

11. The first estimation of the number of moves needed to solve a Rubik's cube was fifty-two, arrived at in July 1981. Then this number gradually decreased, from forty-two in 1990 to twenty-nine in 2000 and twenty-two in 2008, eventually reaching the final number of twenty. See "Mathematics of the Rubik's Cube," Ruwix, http://ruwix.com/the-rubiks-cube/mathematics -of-the-rubiks-cube-permutation-group.

12. The idea that information involves aperiodicity and a multitude of correlations of different lengths is also explored in Douglas Hofstadter's *Gödel, Escher, Bach*. See, for instance, Chapter VI: The Location of Meaning. Douglas R. Hofstadter *Gödel, Escher, Bach: An Eternal Golden Braid* (New York: Basic Books, 1979).

13. In recent years methods inspired by the ideas of information have been used to identify new genes in what was believed to be intergenic material. See Anne-Ruxandra Carvunis et al., "Proto-genes and De Novo Gene Birth," *Nature* 487, no. 7407 (2012): 370–374.

14. See Dave Munger, "A Simple Toy, and What It Says About How We Learn to Mentally Rotate Objects," *Cognitive Daily* blog, September 17, 2008, http://scienceblogs.com/cognitivedaily/2008/09/17/a-simple-toy-and -what-it-says; Helena Örnkloo and Claes von Hofsten, "Fitting Objects into Holes: On the Development of Spatial Cognition Skills," *Developmental Psychology* 43, no. 2 (2007): 404.

CHAPTER 3: THE ETERNAL ANOMALY

1. Thinking about past, present, and future is problematic—although common in movies that feature time travel. Our current understanding of physics tells us that the future does not exist. It is being constructed at every instant. In fact, there is only a present that is being computed constantly from the immediate past in a manner that is not fully predictable. Please note that by saying that the present is constructed from the immediate past we are not denying the influence of information from the distant past. We

are only requiring that information to be physically embodied somewhere in the most immediate past to affect the present.

2. In physics, such equivalence is called *symmetry*. Symmetries can be thought of as changes of variables that do not affect the outcome of a physical model. The time reversal symmetry is as simple as noticing that equations of motion are still valid after we change time t by $-t$. This means that a world in which time runs backward does not contradict the physical principles used to derive these equations of motion, and therefore is valid with respect to them.

3. *Free energy* is a technical concept defined as the energy of a system that can be used to produce work. It excludes thermal energy. Imagine having a bowling ball on a high shelf. The total energy of the system is the thermal energy of the bowling ball (since the temperature is not absolute zero) plus the potential energy of the bowling ball on the shelf. The free energy is just the potential energy of the bowling ball on the shelf.

4. Nobel Media AB, "The Nobel Prize in Chemistry 1977," www .nobelprize.org/nobel_prizes/chemistry/laureates/1977.

5. A whirlpool is an information-rich steady state since the distribution of the velocities of water molecules in a whirlpool is far from random. Yet as Prigogine notes, "For a long time turbulence was identified with disorder or noise. Today we know that this is not the case. Indeed, while turbulent motion appears as irregular or chaotic on the macroscopic scale, it is, on the contrary highly organized in the microscopic scale." Ilya Prigogine and Isabelle Stengers, *Order Out of Chaos: Man's New Dialogue with Nature* (New York: Bantam, 1984), 141.

6. Ilya Prigogine, "Étude thermodynamique des phénomènes irréversibles," PhD thesis, Université Libre de Bruxelles, 1947.

7. L. M. Martyushev and V. D. Seleznev, "Maximum Entropy Production Principle in Physics, Chemistry and Biology," *Physics Reports* 426, no. 1 (2006): 1–45.

8. Ilya Prigogine and Grégoire Nicolis, "Biological Order, Structure and Instabilities," *Quarterly Reviews of Biophysics* 4, nos. 2–3 (1971): 107–148. For a more up-to-date discussion of the connection between statistical physics, order, and life, see Jeremy L. England, "Statistical Physics of Self-Replication," *Journal of Chemical Physics* 139, no. 12 (2013): 121923.

9. This thought experiment is not physically accurate—the whirlpool will stop as you freeze it—but you can run it in your head thanks to the powers of imagination. The purpose of the mental image is primarily illustrative.

10. Certainly the information encoded in the positions of the water molecules will be there, but the one that was contained in their velocities—or momentum—disappeared.

11. The Avery-MacLeod-McCarty experiment from 1944 showing that DNA carries genetic information coincided with the publication of Schrodinger's book, so Schrodinger was not aware that DNA, rather than proteins, carried genetic information.

12. This depends on the scale. We can consider a solid to be frozen when thermal fluctuations are too weak to alter its structure. This is true of a building and a car at room temperature. A protein, on the other hand, lives much more at the edge of order and disorder, since thermal fluctuations are important for a protein to fold but a protein structure is still stable in the face of the thermal fluctuations that take place at room temperature.

13. Technically this is known as a bifurcation. It occurs in systems that have nonlinearities, which come from the fact that the production of some intermediate compounds {M} or outputs {O} require, respectively, combinations of inputs {I} and intermediate states {M}.

14. This is one of the central ideas described in Stuart Kauffman, *The Origins of Order: Self-Organization and Selection in Evolution* (New York: Oxford University Press, 1993), and it is an implication of his model of random Boolean networks.

15. For a more detailed explanation, see Prigogine and Stengers, *Order Out of Chaos,* and Ilya Prigogine and Isabelle Stengers, *The End of Certainty: Time, Chaos, and the New Laws of Nature* (New York: Free Press, 1997).

CHAPTER 4: OUT OF OUR HEADS!

1. Why do I choose a crystal as a metaphor? A crystal is a static ordered arrangement of atoms. When we create products, we create tangible and digital objects that contain a solidified or frozen instantiation of a process that is much more fluid and dynamic: imagination. Once a car is built, it becomes the 2015 model, and it is basically frozen until the next model comes out. The same will be true for this book. Revisions to later editions—if any—will be unable to change the information that was physically embodied in the first edition. In that sense, the products that we create are crystals of imagination; they are static instantiations of our ideas.

2. In economics it is common to describe technology as the ratio of the total economic output obtained from a productive activity (thought of as profit) to the quantity of inputs used in that economic activity (usually described in terms of their costs). This definition, although attractive from a financial perspective, is at odds with the use of the word *technology* by many of the people who build technology. In general, technologists use the word to refer to a packet of information, which can be either tangible (like a microchip) or digital (like a software library) and has the capacity to expand

our ability to do things. Technologies do not just make slower things faster or more efficient. They make the impossible possible, allowing us to do new things. The traditional definition of technology used in economics would imply that a reduction of salaries that does not affect the output produced could be interpreted as an increase in technology, since it involves the same amount of output with less input (an increase in total factor productivity). From the perspective of a technologist, this cannot be seen as an improvement in technology, as it does not increase our ability to do new things.

3. Certainly it is firms, rather than countries, that do the exporting. But since the export basket of a country is the combination of the exports of many firms, here I will discuss exports using countries for simplicity.

4. "Products That Chile Exports to South Korea (2012)," Observatory of Economic Complexity, MIT Media Lab, http://atlas.media.mit.edu/explore /tree_map/hs/export/chl/kor/show/2012.

5. "Products That Chile Imports from South Korea (2012)," Observatory of Economic Complexity, MIT Media Lab, http://atlas.media.mit.edu /explore/tree_map/hs/import/chl/kor/show/2012.

6. According to Angus Maddison's historical GDP estimates, in 1900 Chile had a GDP per capita (in 1990 constant dollars) of $2,194, versus $1,786 for Spain, $2,083 for Sweden and $1,877 for Finland.

7. "Products Exported by Chile (2012)," Observatory of Economic Complexity, MIT Media Lab, http://atlas.media.mit.edu/oi5z2n.

8. Technically, the official estimate for the average Chilean family size is 2.9 people. See www.ministeriodesarrollosocial.gob.cl/casen2009/familia .php.

9. International Energy Agency, "Electricity/Heat in World in 2009," www.iea.org/stats/electricitydata.asp?COUNTRY_CODE=29.

10. Even though oil was used prior to that to power kerosene lamps.

11. Nikola Tesla, *My Inventions* (n.p.: Philovox, 2013).

12. A view of the world in which humans act to maximize utility is logically unsound when combined with its own empirical validation—the idea of revealed preferences. In simple terms, it is easy to understand the circularity of the argument by considering separately the theory (utility maximization) and its empirical validation (individual choices reflect individual preferences). If we consider the idea that individuals maximize utility to be a hypothesis, then to test it we need a test in which one of the possible outcomes is to observe that individuals do not maximize utility. Revealed preferences is not that test, since it assumes that the actions taken by an individual are always aligned with the choice that maximizes her preference, and hence, is a test that by construction cannot result in an individual making a choice that does not maximize utility. So together, the ideas of

utility maximization and revealed preferences cannot be considered a proof of individuals acting in self-interest, or of anything else for that matters. Francis Fukuyama points this out as well. When referring to utility maximization and the attitude of economists toward this idea, he writes: "Some economists try to get around this problem by broadening the definition of utility beyond pleasure of money to take account of other motivations such as the 'psychic pleasure' one receives for 'doing the right thing,' or the pleasure people can take in other people's consumption. Economists assert that one can know what is useful by their choices—hence their concept 'revealed preference.' The abolitionist dying to end slavery and the investment banker speculating on interest rates are both said to be pursuing 'utility,' the only difference being that the abolitionist's utility is of a psychic sort. At its most extreme, 'utility' becomes a purely formal concept used to describe whatever ends or preferences people pursue. But this type of formal definition of utility reduces the fundamental premise of economics to an assertion that people maximize whatever it is they choose to maximize, a tautology that robs the model of any interest or explanatory power." Francis Fukuyama, *Trust: The Social Virtues and the Creation of Prosperity* (New York: Free Press, 1995), 19.

CHAPTER 5: AMPLIFIERS

1. This echoes ideas from urban activist Jane Jacobs. When Jacobs was asked about the importance of greed and self-interest in the economy, she remarked: "You are leaving out the most important things about economies. You can't have greed unless there is something to be greedy about." Video interview with Jane Jacobs on the nature of economies, https://www.youtube.com/watch?v=UPNPpdBCqzU.

2. George Johnson, *The Ten Most Beautiful Experiments* (New York: Knopf, 2008), 76–86.

3. I have taken the liberty of expanding this example substantially, since in Wiener's book it is not mentioned in a very straightforward way and furthermore is woven into a weird Cold War political argument. Norbert Wiener, *The Human Use of Human Beings: Cybernetics and Society* (Boston: Houghton Mifflin, 1950).

CHAPTER 6: THIS TIME, IT'S PERSONAL

1. The question of which industries locate where and why has given rise to at least four theoretical streams of literature: the literature on industrial clusters, the "new economic geography" (which is the neoclassical stream of this literature), the economic geography literature focusing on institutions and culture, and the evolutionary economic geography literature. One could

argue that these different strands of literature reflect academic alliances and divisions, but I will describe them not in terms of academic divisions but in terms of how they conceptualize sources of economic advantage and the patterns of industrial diversification and specialization found in different locations.

First I will consider the approaches that emphasize the role of individuals. These include the neoclassical approaches of Paul Krugman, Masahisa Fujita, and Anthony Venables. As described by Krugman, the new economic geography is a theoretical effort to figure out why industries would locate in a certain location (agglomeration). The goal of the new economic geography is to develop general-equilibrium models that are completely endogenous. These are models where constraints on both money and resources are honored, and where supply, demand, and population are determined endogenously from the models. To achieve its goal, the new economic geography uses a number of theoretical tricks that help make these models tractable. These include the use of Dixit and Stiglitz's monopolistic competition model (Avinash K. Dixit and Joseph E. Stiglitz, "Monopolistic Competition and Optimum Product Diversity," *American Economic Review* 67, no. 3 [1977]: 297–308) or Paul Samuelson's iceberg costs (Paul A. Samuelson, "The Transfer Problem and Transport Costs, II: Analysis of Effects of Trade Impediments," *Economic Journal* 64, no. 254 [1954]: 264–289). Yet the highly stylized nature of the models has limited their empirical validation. In fact, early efforts to calibrate the models found that these have a tendency to agglomerate that was stronger than that observed in the real economy (see, for example, Paul Krugman, "What's New About the New Economic Geography?," *Oxford Review of Economic Policy* 14, no. 2 [1998]: 7–17), and more recent attempts to find evidence have generated more discussion than answers (see, for example, Stephen J. Redding, "The Empirics of the New Economic Geography," *Journal of Regional Science* 50, no. 1 [2010]: 297–311).

Another approach that hinges on individuals, albeit differently from the approach followed by the new economic geographers, is the work of urban theorist Richard Florida. Florida has argued forcefully that the competitiveness of urban agglomerations hinges largely on their ability to attract creative individuals (Richard Florida, *The Rise of the Creative Class and How It's Transforming Work, Leisure, Community, and Everyday Life* (New York: Basic Books, 2002]).

Other approaches focus not on the role of individuals but on the properties of regions or of the networks of firms that locate in these regions. One strand of this literature focuses on industrial clusters associated mostly with the Harvard Business School professor Michael Porter (see, for example, Michael E. Porter, *On Competition* [Boston: Harvard Business School Press, 2008]). This literature, however, can also be traced back—albeit in a more rudimentary form—to Alfred Marshall's nineteenth-century work on industrial districts (for example, *Principles of Economics* [London: Macmillan, 1890]). Porter discusses industrial clusters in terms of demand conditions, specific factors, strategy, and related industries. With the last item he emphasizes the importance of local value chains, echoing somehow the work of Alfred Hirschman on backward linkages (for example, Albert O. Hirschman, "The Strategy of Economic Development," in A. N. Agarwal and S. P. Singh, eds., *Accelerating Investment in Developing Economies* [London: Oxford University Press, 1969].)

Approaches emphasizing the role of regions include those of economic geographers, who have contributed to explaining differences between regions in terms of properties of these regions. This work includes the institutional literature explaining differences in the composition of industrial clusters based on differences in features of a location, in particular their social and formal institutions. (See, for example, Francis Fukuyama, *Trust: The Social Virtues and the Creation of Prosperity* [New York: Free Press, 1995]; AnnaLee Saxenian, *Regional Advantage* [Cambridge, MA: Harvard University Press, 1996]; and Daron Acemoglu and James A. Robinson, *Why Nations Fail: The Origins of Power, Prosperity, and Poverty* [New York: Crown Business, 2012].) For instance, an argument explaining differences between the composition and success of two industrial clusters in terms of the culture of the people located in them (religion, family orientation, etc.), or the formal rules that are in place, would fall into the categories of theories based on social or formal institutions, respectively. Finally, there is the literature on evolutionary economic geography, which builds on considerations of how knowledge is accumulated in firms and networks of firms. This literature builds on the ideas of routines introduced by Richard R. Nelson and Sidney G. Winter (*An Evolutionary Theory of Economic Change* [Cambridge, MA: Harvard University Press, 1982]) and emphasizes the tacit nature of the knowledge embedded in firms, the ability of firms to absorb tacit knowledge, and the recombination of knowledge, which is inspired by ideas from Schumpeter (for example, Joseph A. Schumpeter, *The Theory of Economic Development: An Inquiry into Profits, Capital, Credit, Interest, and the Business Cycle* [Cambridge, MA: Harvard University Press, 1934]). A good review comparing the evolutionary economic geography literature to other approaches is Ron A. Boschma and Koen Frenken, "Why Is Economic Geography Not an Evolutionary Science? Towards an Evolutionary Economic Geography," *Journal of Economic Geography* 6, no. 3 (2006): 273–302.

2. The idea that economic actors need to figure out how to make what they make challenged some assumptions that—while naive—had become engrained in economics. Economists Ricardo Hausmann and Dani Rodrik call attention to the fact that entrepreneurs need to discover the cost of producing at a given location; these discovery costs were absent from mainstream economic models (Ricardo Hausmann and Dani Rodrik, "Economic Development as Self-Discovery," *Journal of Development Economics* 72, no. 2 (2003): 603–633).

3. Michael Polanyi, *The Tacit Dimension* (Garden City, NY: Doubleday, 1966), 4.

4. Walter Powell, "Neither Market nor Hierarchy," *Research in Organizational Behavior* 12 (1990): 295–336. A detailed discussion of tacit knowledge can be found in Richard R. Nelson and Sidney G. Winter, *An Evolutionary Theory of Economic Change* (Cambridge, MA: Harvard University Press, 1982), ch. 4, sec. 2.

5. For a seminal introduction to social learning see Albert Bandura, *Social Learning Theory* (Englewood Cliffs, NJ: Prentice-Hall, 1977), esp. 305–316. For a more recent example using experiments to show the empirical prevalence and advantage of social learning, see Luke Rendell et al., "Why Copy Others? Insights from the Social Learning Strategies Tournament," *Science* 328, no. 5975 (2010): 208–213.

6. Strictly speaking, learning by having access to the same facilities, or environment, is not a form of social learning, but context-based learning.

7. Of course there are individual-level differences in the cognitive capacities of people, and one might argue that some people can carry more personbytes than others. However, the differences in cognitive capacities between individuals are dwarfed by the differences between the knowledge that the brightest individual can hold and that which society holds collectively. Hence, to understand collective processes involving complex products or networks of people, the idea of a personbyte as a basic unit of productive knowledge is useful.

8. I would like to note that, as an economic function, the ability of networks of humans to accumulate large volumes of knowledge is different from the economic functions that are often emphasized when discussing the economic relevance of social networks. The traditional channels by which social networks are said to affect economies are information transfer, sources of reward and punishment, and repositories of trust. As the sociologist Mark Granovetter explains: "Social structure, especially in the form of social networks, affects economic outcomes for three main reasons. First, social networks affect the flow and the quality of information. Much information is subtle, nuanced and difficult to verify, so actors do not believe

impersonal sources and instead rely on people they know. Second, social networks are an important source of reward and punishment, since these are often magnified in their impact when coming from others personally known. Third, trust, by which I mean the confidence that others will do the 'right' thing despite a clear balance of incentives to the contrary, emerges, if it does, in the context of a social network" (Mark Granovetter, "The Impact of Social Structure on Economic Outcomes," *Journal of Economic Perspective* 19, no. 1 [2005]: 33–50). I review more of the literature connecting social networks and economic networks in Chapter 8.

9. We say that social learning slows down the accumulation of knowledge because finding opportunities for social learning is hard and costly. In general, the existence of social learning speeds up other learning—it is faster to learn from experts. The point here is that the need for social learning slows down knowledge accumulation because it is hard for individuals to find the social learning opportunities they require to acquire each specific chunk of knowledge.

10. A great book eloquently describing the role of genes on human behavior is Steven Pinker's *The Blank Slate: The Modern Denial of Human Nature* (New York: Penguin, 2003).

11. During the last couple of decades the political scientists and biologists working in the field of genopolitics have amassed an impressive amount of evidence connecting political preferences and genetics. These studies have hinged largely on exploiting data on identical and nonidentical twins, which they have matched with voter records and political party affiliations. Certainly this is a controversial area of research, in part because most people are not ready to accept that genes can affect their political choices, and in part because some political scientists have gone as far as calling the findings irrelevant even if true; see Larry Bartels, "Your Genes Influence Your Political Views. So What?," *Monkey Cage* blog, *Washington Post,* November 12, 2013. For a popular description of the field of genopolitics, I recommend John Hibbing, "Why Biology Belongs in the Study of Politics," *Monkey Cage* blog, *Washington Post,* November 27, 2013. For academic papers connecting political views to genetics, see John R. Alford, Carolyn L. Funk, and John R. Hibbing, "Are Political Orientations Genetically Transmitted?," *American Political Science Review* 99, no. 2 (2005): 153–167; Carolyn L. Funk et al., "Genetic and Environmental Transmission of Political Orientations," *Political Psychology* 34, no. 6 (2013): 805–819; Christian Kandler, Wiebke Bleidorn, and Rainer Riemann, "Left or Right? Sources of Political Orientation: The Roles of Genetic Factors, Cultural Transmission, Assortative Mating, and Personality," *Journal of Personality and Social Psychology* 102, no. 3 (2012): 633. For papers focusing on genetics and political participation,

see James H. Fowler, Laura A. Baker, and Christopher T. Dawes, "Genetic Variation in Political Participation," *American Political Science Review* 102, no. 2 (2008): 233–248; James H. Fowler and Christopher T. Dawes, "Two Genes Predict Voter Turnout," *Journal of Politics* 70, no. 3 (2008): 579–594; James H. Fowler and Christopher T. Dawes, "In Defense of Genopolitics," *American Political Science Review* 107, no. 2 (2013): 362–374.

12. Brett Stetka, "What Do Great Musicians Have in Common? DNA," *Scientific American,* August 4, 2014.

13. The fact that the genetic variation between individuals is much larger than the genetic variation between groups is a key argument to fend off racist and eugenic arguments. This explanation is key to the line of argumentation advanced in Pinker, *The Blank Slate.*

14. Speculating about the knowledge- and information-carrying capacity of the human brain is an interesting exercise. Among the first ones to perform this exercise was John von Neumann, the Hungarian polymath who became interested in computers while working on the Manhattan Project. Some of his speculations on the topic are presented in his *The Computer and the Brain* (New Haven, CT: Yale University Press, 1958). There, Neumann notes that the architecture of the brain is fundamentally different from that of computers. Computers are built on transistors, which take two inputs to produce one output, while brains are built on neurons, which can take up to tens of thousands of inputs to produce a single output. These differences are important, since the frequency of the brain, which he noted to be about 100 Hz, needs to be scaled by a factor that considers such multiplicity of inputs.

We can do a simple back-of-the-envelope calculation for the storage capacity of the brain by looking at the number of neurons and synapses in a normal human brain: approximately 10^{10} neurons and 10^{14} synapses (with an average of 10,000 synapses per neuron). One naive estimate of the information storage capacity of the brain would be to consider each of these synapses to be a bit, resulting in a figure of 100 terabytes. A more ambitious yet also naive estimate would be to consider each of the existing synapses as 1's and the possible but not materialized synapses as 0's. If we assume that each of the 10,000 synapses of a neuron are chosen from a set of 100,000 possible synapses, then the information storage capacity of the brain would be estimated at 1,000 terabytes or one petabyte.

CHAPTER 7: LINKS ARE NOT FREE

1. Greg Grandin, *Fordlandia: The Rise and Fall of Henry Ford's Forgotten Jungle City* (New York: Metropolitan Books, 2009).

2. Certainly one can argue that most companies get started by small teams, such as that of Daimler and Benz or Jobs and Wozniak, and hence that in reality few personbytes are involved in the production of these goods. While it is true that an early Daimler vehicle or an Apple I can be built by a small group of people, this is not true for the later, more sophisticated models. As companies scale and move into more complex products, they accumulate larger volumes of productive knowledge. So if we consider the creation and worldwide distribution of the 2014 Mercedes 300 to be a different product from the building of a few custom engine-powered carriages, then we will need to accept that for these more complex products we need more personbytes, even if they appear to belong to the same category.

3. It would be naive to conclude that all divisions between firms are the result of limits in their ability to accumulate knowledge. The size of most firms is constrained by other forces that are much simpler to understand, the most prominent one being the number of people they can afford. Yet, even firms with infinitely deep pockets will at some point bump into a finite knowledge carrying capacity, which (in agreement with Ronald Coase's theory of the firm, which we will review later in this chapter) will be expressed in the price difference between doing an activity internally and hiring it from the market.

4. Ronald H. Coase, "The Nature of the Firm," *Economica* 4, no. 16 (1937): 386–405. We could also use as a starting point John R. Commons' "Institutional Economics," *American Economic Review* 21 (1931): 648–657. Transaction cost theory, institutional economics, and its younger and uninspiredly named cousin, new institutional economics, study the interactions between economic agents, the decisions that push agents to interact, and the contracts and governance structures mediating those interactions. An introduction to the literature is also available in Howard A. Shelanski, and Peter G. Klein. "Empirical Research in Transaction Cost Economics: A Review and Assessment," *Journal of Law, Economics, and Organization* 11, no. 2 (1995): 335–361.

5. This story comes from Ronald Coase, "The Institutional Structure of Production," *American Economic Review* 82, no. 4 (1992): 713–719.

6. For those who are not familiar with the quote, it is "Everything should be made as simple as possible, but not simpler." Details on the history of this quote, including the debate about whether it was actually voiced by Einstein, can be found at http://quoteinvestigator.com/2011/05/13/einstein -simple.

7. It is also reasonable to consider simpler theories that limit the size of firms. For instance, a relational view of the hiring process would limit the

size of the firm by its revenue, by assuming that people hire other people as long as they can afford to.

8. Miyoung Kim, "Analysis: Friend and Foe; Samsung, Apple Won't Want to Damage Parts Deal," Reuters, August 27, 2012.

9. Walter Isaacson, *Steve Jobs* (New York: Simon and Schuster, 2011).

10. For those curious about the iPad games, I would recommend, in addition to the three games mentioned in the main text, XCom: Enemy Unknown, Civilization Revolution, Sim City, Waking Mars, Cyto, and Osmos.

11. Oliver Williamson, "Transaction-Cost Economics: The Governance of Contractual Relations," *Journal of Law and Economics* 22, no. 2 (1979): 233–261.

12. He labels this "investment characteristic."

13. In a 1997 paper, Brian Uzzi studies in detail the embeddedness of links among garment manufacturers and their suppliers. See Brian Uzzi, "Social Structure and Competition in Interfirm Networks: The Paradox of Embeddedness," *Administrative Science Quarterly* 42, no. 1 (1997): 35–67.

14. "Free Exchange: Down Towns," *The Economist*, August 15, 2013. However, the change in communication technologies has been mostly qualitative. To estimate the change in costs fairly, we would need to know how much a late nineteenth-century industrialist would pay for asynchronous technologies such as email, or for a simple Skype call. And it is interesting to note that, as James Gleick describes beautifully in *The Information: A History, a Theory, a Flood* (New York: Pantheon, 2011), the French invention of the telegraph was based on contraptions whose arm positions were used to transmit information. This mechanical telegraph long predated the electric telegraph that we are more familiar with, and which became the standard image that comes to mind when using the word.

15. Coase, "The Institutional Structure of Production," highlights the standardization role of money as its most fundamental yet overlooked property.

16. Currently the standard license to manufacture USB devices costs USD $4,000 a year (http://www.usb.org/developers/vendor).

17. Some standards are regional, such as the voltage we use and the shape of our outlets, while others are surprisingly global, such as the sizes of bicycle tires and the heights of chairs and tables. The Web is an excellent example of a global system built on top of a growing ensemble of standards, including protocols such as TCP/IP and Web standards such as CSS and HTML. Even money is an example of a standardization technology that emerged together with the rise of commerce and our need to simplify the burden of economic transactions. Friedrich Hayek famously pointed this out in a 1945 paper ("The Use of Knowledge in Society," *American*

Economic Review 35, no. 4 [1945]: 519–530). There, Hayek identified money as an information revelation mechanism that helped uncover information regarding the availability and demand of goods in different parts of the economy.

18. J. C. Scott, *Seeing like a State: How Certain Schemes to Improve the Human Condition Have Failed* (New Haven, CT: Yale University Press, 1998).

19. M. Pagel, "Human Language as a Culturally Transmitted Replicator," *Nature Reviews Genetics* 10, no. 6 (2009): 405–415.

20. Ronen Shahar, Bruno Goncalves, Kevin Hu, Alessandro Vespignani, Steven Pinker, and César A. Hidalgo, "Links That Speak: The Global Language Network and Its Association to Global Fame," *Proceedings of the National Academy of Sciences*, (10.1073/pnas.1410931111(2014)).

21. G. F. Davis, *Managed by the Markets: How Finance Re-shaped America* (New York: Oxford University Press, 2009).

22. L. P. Casalino et al., "What Does It Cost Physician Practices to Interact with Health Insurance Plans?," *Health Affairs* 28, no. 4 (2009): w533–w543.

23. Henry J. Aaron, "The Costs of Health Care Administration in the United States and Canada: Questionable Answers to a Questionable Question," *New England Journal of Medicine* 349, no. 8 (2003): 801–803; S. Woolhandler, T. Campbell, and D. U. Himmelstein, "Costs of Health Care Administration in the United States and Canada," *New England Journal of Medicine* 349, no. 8 (2003): 768–775.

24. Woolhandler, Campbell, and Himmelstein, "Costs of Health Care Administration."

25. There were also financial incentives that helped catalyze this dismembering. See Davis, *Managed by the Markets*.

26. Benjamin Ginsberg, *The Fall of the Faculty: The Rise of the All-Administrative University and Why It Matters* (Oxford: Oxford University Press, 2011).

27. Woolhandler, Campbell, and Himmelstein, "Costs of Health Care Administration."

Chapter 8: In Links We Trust

1. The latter being an example that if you want economists to consider your point of view, you need to give the surname "capital" to whatever aspect of the world you are looking to incorporate into the economic discussion!

2. The economic importance of social networks and trust, however, has been hard to reconcile with mainstream descriptions of the economy. Traditional (neoclassical) descriptions of the economy have a tendency to overemphasize the ability of the markets and formal institutions to shape social structure, and hence such descriptions have a tendency to promote

an undersocialized view of humans. The critique that economists have of social theory is exactly the opposite—that sociologists have a tendency to assume an oversocialized individual. Surprisingly, the latter critique was made famous by a sociologist, Dennis Wrong, who criticized the oversocialized view of individuals advanced by his colleagues in the early 1960s; see his "The Oversocialized Conception of Man in Modern Sociology," *American Sociological Review* 26, no. 2 (1961): 183–193. Here, however, I will use the description of both critiques presented by James Coleman in his seminal paper on social capital, "Social Capital in the Creation of Human Capital," *American Journal of Sociology* 94 (1988): S95–S120.

There are two broad intellectual streams in the description and explanation of social action. One, characteristic of the work of most sociologists, sees the actor as socialized and action as governed by social norms, rules, and obligations. The principal virtues of this intellectual stream lie in its ability to describe action in social context and to explain the way action is shaped, constrained, and redirected by social context.

The other intellectual stream, characteristic of the work of most economists, sees the actor as having goals independently arrived at, as acting independently, as wholly self-interested. Its principal virtue lies in having a principle of action, that of maximizing utility. This principle of action, together with a single empirical generalization (declining marginal utility), has generated the extensive growth of neoclassical economic theory, as well as the growth of political philosophy of several varieties: utilitarianism, contractarianism, and natural rights. . . . Both these intellectual streams have serious defects. The sociological stream has what may be a fatal flaw as a theoretical enterprise: the actor has no 'engine of action'. The actor is shaped by the environment, but there are no internal springs of action that give the actor a purpose or direction. . . .

The economic stream, on the other hand, flies in the face of empirical reality: persons' actions are shaped, redirected, constrained by the social context; norms, interpersonal trust, social networks, and social organization are important in the functioning not only of the society but also of the economy.

Yet another point of friction between social theory and economic theory has been in the attempts by economists to develop models that explain social structure and institutions as the outcome of dynamic or evolutionary processes where the history of social interactions plays no role. In the words of Mark Granovetter: "The general story told by members of [the new institutional economics] group of thought is that social institutions and arrangements previously thought to be the adventitious result of legal, historical, social or political forces are better viewed as the efficient solution to certain economic problems. The tone is similar to that of structural-functional sociology of the 1940s to the 1960s" (Mark Granovetter, "Economic Action and Social Structure: The Problem of Embeddedness," *American Journal of Sociology* 91, no. 3 [1985]: 481–510). Francis Fukuyama criticizes institutional economics in a similar light: "Most economists have assumed that group formation does not depend on ethical habit but arises naturally following the establishment of legal institutions like property rights and contract law"; Francis Fukuyama, *Trust: The Social Virtues and the Creation of Prosperity* (New York: Free Press, 1995).

3. Mark Granovetter, *Getting a Job: A Study of Contacts and Careers* (Cambridge, MA: Harvard University Press, 1974).

4. Ibid.

5. Nelson D. Schwartz, "In Hiring, a Friend in Need Is a Prospect, Indeed," *New York Times*, January 27, 2013.

6. In his now classic book on social capital, *Bowling Alone*, Robert Putnam also echoes some of Granovetter's findings by highlighting the economic importance of social networks in labor markets and finance. He reviews a number of examples including this: "In Los Angeles two-thirds of white and black women who had looked for a job in the past five years landed their latest or current position with the help of someone they knew in the firm." When it comes to finance, he notes that of the 70 percent of Korean entrepreneurs who used debt financing to start their enterprise, "41 percent got their money from family and 24 percent from friends (compared with 37 percent from a financial institution)." Putnam, *Bowling Alone: The Collapse and Revival of American Community* (New York: Simon and Schuster, 2000), 320.

7. Granovetter, "Economic Action and Social Structure."

8. Fukuyama, *Trust*, 49.

9. Putnam differentiates between bonding and bridging social capital. Bonding social capital is the one taking place within densely connected networks, where people look out for each other, while bridging social capital is that by which people can easily reach distant parts of the network (Ronald Burt's structural holes). As Putnam puts it: "Bonding social capital constitutes a kind of sociological superglue, whereas bridging social capital provides a sociological WD-40." Putnam, *Bowling Alone*, 23.

10. Coren L. Apicella et al., "Social Networks and Cooperation in Hunter-Gatherers," *Nature* 481, no. 7382 (2012): 497–501.

11. Ibid. To test cooperation they used a variation of a public-goods game. This means that cooperation was assessed not by self-reporting but as the behavioral outcome of a pseudo-recreational activity where individuals could choose to behave in a cooperative manner or not.

12. Fukuyama, *Trust*, 352.

13. Coleman, "Social Capital in the Creation of Human Capital."

14. AnnaLee Saxenian, "Inside-Out: Regional Networks and Industrial Adaptation in Silicon Valley and Route 128," *Cityscape*, May 1996, 41–60.

15. For a discussion on adaptability see also Walter Powell, "Neither Market nor Hierarchy: Network Forms of Organization," in Michael J. Handel, ed., *The Sociology of Organizations: Classic, Contemporary, and Critical Readings* (Thousand Oaks, CA: Sage Publications, 2003), 104–117.

16. As the sociologist Walter Powell noted, "Networks . . . possess some degree of comparative advantage in coping with an environment that places a premium on innovation and customized products" (ibid.). Networks are more adaptable than hierarchies because partnerships and coalitions are a faster means of adaptability than internal development (see Michael E. Porter and Mark B. Fuller, "Coalitions and Global Strategy," *Competition in Global Industries* 1, no. 10 [1986]: 315–343), but also because they are better at communicating information that is crucial for the members of a regional cluster to learn about changes in markets and technologies.

17. Schwartz, "In Hiring, a Friend in Need Is a Prospect, Indeed."

18. Putnam, *Bowling Alone*, ch. 23.

19. Fukuyama, *Trust*, 351. It is also worth noting that social institutions are not just geographically circumscribed but tend to travel with immigrants, at least for a few generations. As a pair of economists have found, the strength of family ties has effects on family size, social mobility and the participation of women in the labor force that survive in immigrants even after a couple of generations. Alberto Alesina and Paola Giuliano, "The Power of the Family," *Journal of Economic Growth* 15, no. 2 (2010): 93–125.

20. Putnam, *Bowling Alone*, 345.

21. Fukuyama, *Trust*, 113.

22. Ibid., 62.

23. Barry Wellman et al., "Does the Internet Increase, Decrease, or Supplement Social Capital? Social Networks, Participation, and Community Commitment," *American Behavioral Scientist* 45, no. 3 (2001): 436–455.

CHAPTER 9: THE EVOLUTION OF ECONOMIC COMPLEXITY

1. See P. M. Visscher, "Sizing Up Human Height Variation," *Nature Genetics* 40, no. 5 (2008): 489–490; G. Lettre et al., "Identification of Ten Loci Associated with Height Highlights New Biological Pathways in Human Growth," *Nature Genetics* 40, no. 5 (2008): 584–591.

2. I am not assuming that the knowledge required to make a product is located in only one place. As we saw in the previous chapter, often this knowledge is dismembered and distributed among global networks of firms. Yet the interactions of these firms are mediated by transactions involving intermediate products. So when we observe a place (a country, say, or a city) manufacturing cars, we are not assuming anything other than the knowledge of how to assemble cars, since the knowledge required to process rubber, smelt metal, or build engines could well be located elsewhere.

3. The literature on nestedness in ecology is extensive, dealing both with the presence-absence matrices connecting species to their habitats and with mutualistic networks such as those connecting flowers to their pollinators. A recent review of this literature, and a place to get started for those interested in the topic, is W. Ulrich, M. Almeida-Neto, and N. J. Gotelli, "A Consumer's Guide to Nestedness Analysis," *Oikos* 118, no. 1 (2009): 3–17.

4. Here we consider a country to be an exporter of a product if its per-capita exports of that product are at least 25 percent of the world's average per capita exports of that product. This allows us to control for the size of the product's global market and the size of the country's population.

5. In the case of Honduras and Argentina the probability of the observed overlap (what is known academically as its *p*-value) is 4.4×10^{-4}. The same probability is 2×10^{-2} for the overlap observed between Honduras and the Netherlands and 4×10^{-3} for the overlap observed between Argentina and the Netherlands.

6. César A. Hidalgo and Ricardo Hausmann, "The Building Blocks of Economic Complexity," *Proceedings of the National Academy of Sciences* 106, no. 26 (2009): 10570–10575.

7. The idea of related varieties is popular in the literature of regional economic development and strategic management. See, for example, Koen Frenken, Frank Van Oort, and Thijs Verburg, "Related Variety, Unrelated Variety and Regional Economic Growth," *Regional Studies* 41, no. 5 (2007): 685–697; Ron Boschma and Simona Iammarino, "Related Variety, Trade Linkages, and Regional Growth in Italy," *Economic Geography* 85, no. 3 (2009): 289–311.

8. Technically, this is because the horse and a zebra share a more recent ancestor than do the horse and the crocodile.

9. Data on colocation or coexports work okay at large spatial scales but do not work well at small spatial scales (neighborhood level), since at that scale demand considerations rather than constraints in the supply help drive much of the colocation. For instance, we would not consider the co-location of a hair salon and a bakery on a neighborhood corner to be evidence of similarities in the knowledge used by these industries. A simpler explanation here is that these are services that serve a demand that is highly

localized—people are not likely to travel across town just to get bread or to get their hair cut. Industries that export, on the other hand, serve larger areas and are therefore under a stronger pressure to find a location that provides them with a knowledge advantage.

10. C. A. Hidalgo, B. Klinger, A. L. Barabási, and R. Hausmann, "The Product Space Conditions the Development of Nations," *Science* 317, no. 5837 (2007): 482–487.

11. See Dataviva.info.

12. F. Neffke, M. Henning, and R. Boschma, "How Do Regions Diversify over Time? Industry Relatedness and the Development of New Growth Paths in Regions." *Economic Geography* 87, no. 3 (2011): 237–265; F. Neffke and M. Henning, "Skill Relatedness and Firm Diversification," *Strategic Management Journal* 34, no. 3 (2013): 297–316; Frank Neffke and Martin Svensson Henning, "Revealed Relatedness: Mapping Industry Space," *Papers in Evolutionary Economic Geography* 8 (2008): 19.

13. But these are not the only ones. Formal mathematical models of this idea can also be used to account for the distribution of diversities, co-location and proximities observed in these matrices (see R. Hausmann and C. A. Hidalgo, "The Network Structure of Economic Output," *Journal of Economic Growth* 16, 4 [2011]: 309–342) as well as the dynamics of these variables over time (I am doing work with Cristian Figueroa on this topic).

Chapter 10: The Sixth Substance

1. The definition of physical capital is technically broader than machinery, however, since it is used to indicate all past production. For example, physical capital can also refer to the stock of grain owned by a flour mill.

2. Adam Smith, *The Wealth of Nations* (London: T. Nelson and Sons, 1887), 116.

3. Ibid.

4. Kuznets originally generated the concept of gross national product (GNP), which was the official metric at the time. Gross domestic product (GDP) displaced GNP as the official metric in the 1990s. GDP considers the production of goods and services within a country. GNP considers the goods and services produced by the citizens of a country, whether or not those goods are produced within the boundaries of the country.

5. Simon Kuznets, "Modern Economic Growth: Findings and Reflections," *American Economic Review* 63, no. 3 (1973): 247–258.

6. Technically, total factor productivity is the residual or error term of the statistical model. Also, economists often refer to total factor productivity as technology, although this is a semantic deformation that is orthogonal to the definition of technology used by anyone who has ever developed a technology. In the language of economics, technology is the ability to do

more—of anything—with the same cost. For inventors of technology, technology is the ability to do something completely new, which often involves the development of a new capacity. As an example, consider a computer and a typewriter. A computer is not a faster typewriter, even if it accelerates the process of typing a document. This is because a computer can be used to do things that you cannot do with typewriters, such as play video games, create 3-D architectural models, and command a 3-D printer. Often, however, inventors use the word *technology* in an even narrower sense, to define particular capacities. For instance, giant magnetoresistance (GMR) is a technology that is used to read information from hard drives; this is different from shingled magnetic recording (SMR), which is a more recent method to read information from hard drives that could help increase the size of hard drives to tens of terabytes.

7. By similar, I mean that they are based on the mathematical idea of coupled ordinary differential equations.

8. Wassily Leontief, "Theoretical Assumptions and Non-observed Facts," *American Economic Review* 61, no. 1 (1971): 1–7.

9. Michael Porter, *On Competition* (Boston: Harvard Business School Press, 2008), 188. Other economists that have made calls to steer away from aggregation include Esther Duflo, Abhijit Banerjee, and Robert Lucas. Duflo and Banerjee show evidence that differences in productivity within an economy are large enough to render the idea of an aggregate production function nonsensical; Abhijit V. Banerjee and Esther Duflo, "Growth Theory Through the Lens of Development Economics," in *Handbook of Economic Growth*, vol. 1, ed. Philippe Aghion, 473–552 (Amsterdam: Elsevier, 2005). Robert Lucas—a Nobel Prize winner—argued that "a successful theory of development (or anything else) has to involve more than aggregative modeling." In fact, in agreement with Leontief, Lucas argued that this disaggregation needed to incorporate increases in the diversity of products being made by the economy: "A growth miracle sustained for a period of decades must involve the continual introduction of new goods, not merely continual learning on a fixed set of goods." R. E. Lucas, "On the Mechanics of Economic Development," *Journal of Monetary Economics* 22, no. 1 (1988): 3–42.

10. Paul M. Romer, "Endogenous Technological Change," *Journal of Political Economy* 98, no. 5 (1990): S71–S102.

11. N. G. Mankiw, D. Romer, and D. N. Weil, "A Contribution to the Empirics of Economic Growth," *Quarterly Journal of Economics* 107, no. 2 (1992): 407–437.

12. They used the average percentage of the working-age population in secondary school for the period 1960–1985.

13. A. W. Woolley, C. F. Chabris, A. Pentland, N. Hashmi, and T. W. Malone, "Evidence for a Collective Intelligence Factor in the Performance

of Human Groups," *Science* 29, vol. 330, no. 6004 (2010): 686–688, http://www.sciencemag.org/content/330/6004/686.

14. Ronald S. Burt, *Brokerage and Closure: An Introduction to Social Capital* (Oxford: Oxford University Press, 2005).

15. For work on bridging social capital, see Ronald S. Burt, *Structural Holes: The Social Structure of Competition* (Cambridge, MA: Harvard University Press, 2009); Ronald S. Burt, "The Contingent Value of Social Capital," *Administrative Science Quarterly* 42, no. 2 (1997): 339–365; Ronald S. Burt, "Secondhand Brokerage: Evidence on the Importance of Local Structure for Managers, Bankers, and Analysts," *Academy of Management Journal* 50, no. 1 (2007): 119–148; Alex Pentland, *Social Physics: How Good Ideas Spread: The Lessons from a New Science* (New York: Penguin, 2014).

16. John F. Heliwell and Robert D. Putnam, "Economic Growth and Social Capital in Italy," *Eastern Economic Journal* 21, 3 (1995): 295–307; Stephen Knack and Philip Keefer, "Does Social Capital Have an Economic Payoff? A Cross-Country Investigation," *Quarterly Journal of Economics* 112, no. 4 (1997): 1251–1288; Paul J. Zak and Stephen Knack, "Trust and Growth," *Economic Journal* 111, no. 470 (2001): 295–321.

17. I found this cartoon on Facebook and have seen it go viral several times. Unfortunately, I could not locate a source to add the appropriate reference.

18. Also, it assumes that prices reveal the interactions between people's needs and the availability of a good—that is, supply and demand force prices to reveal the value of goods.

19. Leontief dedicated a large part of his life to the production of input-output matrices, which connect industries that buy inputs from one another. Leontief wanted to create a description of the economy that went beyond the aggregate gauges that we usually see in the dashboard, such as GDP. His intention was to create a description of the economy that allowed us to see "under the hood," so to speak.

For the understanding that must precede any constructive action it is necessary to penetrate below the surface of global statistics and such round terms as "development." Each economic system—even that of an underdeveloped country—has a complicated internal structure. Its performance is determined by the mutual relations of its differentiated component parts, just as the motion of the hands of a clock is governed by the gears inside.

Leontief was adamant at pushing this view, which he considered opposite to the use of aggregates:

"Gross national product," "Total output," "Value added by manufacture," "Personal consumption expenditures," "Federal Government expenditures," "Exports"—these headings in the book of national accounts describe the familiar external features of the economic system. In recent years the students and the managers of the system have been confronted with many questions that cannot even be clearly posed in such aggregative terms. To answer them one must now look "under the hood" at the inside workings of the system.

To bring his ideas to life, Leontief had to fight not only his colleagues but also the technology available at the time. Leontief's view included the production of input-output matrices, which were computationally too intensive for the computers of the 1950s and 1960s. Still, as early as 1965, he was able to produce matrices for the United States that included as many as eighty-one different sectors. Leontief's vision, however, was not fully carried on by his successors. As computers became more powerful and technological constraints relaxed, input-output matrices did not became substantially more disaggregate. The US input-output matrices that are now made available yearly include as few as sixty-nine industries; every five years the United States produces a matrix that disaggregates these economic links into 388 categories. In the age of Google and the Human Genome Project, our fingerprinting of economic systems is still not much better than the one Leontief advanced in the middle of the twentieth century.

20. For a mathematical description of the method and its relation to a mathematical model and related literature, I recommend starting with César A. Hidalgo and Ricardo Hausmann, "The Building Blocks of Economic Complexity," *Proceedings of the National Academy of Sciences* 106, no. 26 (2009): 10570–10575; C. A. Hidalgo, "The Dynamics of Economic Complexity and the Product Space over a 42-Year Period," working paper 189, Center for International Development, Harvard University, 2009; Ricardo Hausmann and César A. Hidalgo, "The Network Structure of Economic Output," *Journal of Economic Growth* 16, no. 4 (2011): 309–342; Ricardo Hausmann and César A. Hidalgo, *The Atlas of Economic Complexity: Mapping Paths to Prosperity* (Cambridge, MA: MIT Press, 2014).

21. In the economics literature the dynamics of wage and prices equilibration is known as equilibrium. When the equilibration affects the entire market, it is known as general equilibrium. When it affects parts of the market, as in these examples, is known as partial equilibrium.

22. For a colloquial account of the Shenzhen ecosystem, see Joichi Ito, "Shenzen Trip Report: Visiting the World's Manufacturing Ecosystem," *Pulse* blog, LinkedIn, August 17, 2014, https://www.linkedin.com/pulse

/article/20140817060936-1391-shenzhen-trip-report-visiting-the-world
-s-manufacturing-ecosystem.

Chapter 11: The Marriage of Knowledge, Knowhow, and Information

1. Jared M. Diamond, *Guns, Germs and Steel: The Fates of Human Societies* (New York: Random House, 1998).

2. Greg Grandin, *Fordlandia: The Rise and Fall of Henry Ford's Forgotten Jungle City* (New York: Metropolitan Books, 2009).

Chapter 12: The Evolution of Physical Order, from Atoms to Economies

1. And if you provide such an environment with the flow of energy needed to generate and support the growth of information, you will also be elevating its temperature.

INDEX

Aboriginal groups' loss of
  knowhow, 169–170
Adobe, 92
Aggregation, economic growth
  models and, 147–148, 162
Airbus, 122
Akerlof, George, xiv–xv
Altruism, familial networks and,
  121
AMD, 92
American Economic Association,
  147
Ant colonies, 70–71
Aperiodicity of biological
  molecules, 34
Apple, 92, 120, 142
Apple products, 49–50
Apples (fruit), as products, 49–50
Argentina, exports, 132
Atari, 142
Atomic theory, Boltzmann and,
  xi–xii, xiii
Augmentation of human capacities,
  via products, 65–71

Balance of trade, balance of
  imagination and, 52–55
Barabási, László, 109–110
Barbie doll manufacturing
  network, 101–102
Barcelona football team, 73
Biological organisms, knowhow
  embodied in, 166–168
Biology, information and, xiv. See
  also DNA
Birth, as time travel, 3–5
Blek, 92
Blue-collar workers, social
  networks and access to
  employment, 113
Boltzmann, Elsa, xi
Boltzmann, Ludwig, 9, 28, 30
  atomic theory, xi–xii, xiii, 18
  entropy and, xx, 14, 15–17
  origins of physical order and,
    xii–xiii, xvii, xviii, xxi
Bonding social capital, 150–151
Bosch, Carl, 58
Bowling Alone (Putnam), 121, 135

Boyden, Ed, 50, 51, 61
Brain-computer interfaces, 51, 61
Brazil
  balance of trade with China, 55,
    56–57
  Fordlandia, 170–171
  industry space in, 139, 141
Bridging social capital, 150–151
Bugatti, information embodied in,
  11–13, 20
Bureaucratic burden, of linking
  large organizations,
  102–104

Capital
  economic growth and, 146
  human, 148–149, 152, 154–156
  physical, 152–156
  See also Social capital
Car manufacturing
  personbytes required in, 88
  River Rouge complex, 87–88,
    89, 105
Carnot, Nicolas, 60
Center for Cancer Systems Biology,
  110
Chaos, information behind, 30–31
Chemical systems, ability to
  process information, 36–37
Chile
  balance of trade with Korea, 52,
    54–55
  economic complexity of,
    157–159
  industry-location matrices, 133
  raw material exports and, 55,
    58–59, 60
China
  balance of trade with Brazil, 55,
    56–57
  economic growth in, 159

migration of manufacturing
  from United States to,
  161–162
Clausius, Rudolf, 27
Coase, Ronald, 90–91, 93, 95, 102,
  106, 108, 117
Coding
  Shannon and, xvii
  study of information and,
    xiii–xiv
Coleman, James, 117–118
Collaborations, establishing firm-
  to-firm, 102–103
Collective limits on accumulation
  of knowledge and knowhow,
  81–83
Communication, products *vs.*,
  67–68
Communication engineering,
  theory of, 13–15
Compaq, 95
Competitive advantage, 147–148
Complex products
  difficulty of creating, 78–79
  geographical bias in creation of,
    77, 83
  networks of firms and, 92–93
  production in diverse countries,
    134–136
Computation
  ability of matter to compute,
    35–37, 41, 176, 177–178, 181
  of information, 13, 14–15,
    23–24
  knowhow and, 6, 7
Computational capacity, of
  economy, 75, 180–181
Computer industry
  French, 122–123
  networked nature of, 92, 105,
    119–120

standards and cost of market interactions, 95, 100

Computers
information processing and, 36
network production of, 92, 105

Computer scientists, information and, xiv

Concorde, 122

Context, value of products and, 63–64

Copper exports, 55, 58–59, 60

Corning, 92

Corsair, 92

Cost
of firm-to-firm links, 91, 93, 94–95, 102–104
interactions, of health care sector, 104
of market interactions, 95, 100–101
of overbureaucratized networks, 103–104, 106
trust and reduction of transaction, 117–118

Crystallized imagination, 43–47, 178–180
differences in countries' ability to create, 79
knowledge and knowhow and, 61
physical capital and, 152
practical applications of, 65–71
products as, 44, 49–55

Cyberneticists, xiv

Daimler, Gottlieb, 60

Darwin, Charles, 27

DataViva, 139

Davis, Gerald, 101

Davy, Humphry, 59

DEC, 95

Deloitte, 113

Demand
crystallized imagination and creation of, 60
as production stimulus, 77–78

Developed countries, level of trust in, 124

Developing countries
exploitation narrative and, 55, 58–59, 60
exploitation of foreign creativity by, 60
level of trust in, 124

DeVito, Danny, 130

Diamond, Jared, 169–170

Diesel, Rudolf, 60

Digital communication technologies, 14

Diversification toward related varieties, 135–136

Diversified economies, 180

Diversity, stock *vs.*, 152–154, 162

Division of labor, 87–88

D-Link, 92

DNA
decoding richness of information contained in, 22–23, 166–168
information embedded in, 5, 34, 176

Doe, Kelvin, 62

Dorset Eskimos, 170

Dynamic steady state, 28–29
irreversibility of time and, 38

Earth
information and uniqueness of, ix–x
singularity of complexity of, xix

Economic complexity, 145–146
export product ubiquity and, 156–162
measuring, 162–163, 180

Economic development
  challenge of, 75
  knowhow and constraints on
    spread of, 169–171
  wealth *vs.*, 60–61
Economic diversification, product
  space and, 137–139
Economic growth, economic
  complexity and, 157–162, 180
Economic growth models, 146–148,
  162
  human capital and, 148–149
  social capital and, 151
Economic order, growth of
  information and evolution
  of, xx–xxi
Economics, idea of information
  and, xiv–xv
Economic sociology, 111–118
  transaction cost theory and,
    117–118
Economic value
  balance of imagination and, 55,
    58–59, 60
  context of product and, 63–64
Economy
  computational capacity of, 75,
    180–181
  describing, 145–146
  diversified, 180
  knowhow embedded in
    networks, 167–169
  products and characterization
    of, 155–162
  quantization principle and, 168
  reproductive limitations of, 168
  social networks and, 111–124
  as system amplifying practical
    use of knowledge/knowhow,
    68, 69, 70
  as system of information
    growth, 8–9, 177–180

Ecosystems, reproductive
  limitations of, 168
Eddington, Arthur, 11
Edison, Thomas Alva, 11, 59, 69
Eigen, Manfred, 18
Einstein, Albert, 25, 28, 40, 90
Electricity, practical uses of, 59–60,
  69
Energy
  creation of objects and, 43, 44, 181
  information and, 175, 177
  information processing and, 43
Engineers, information and, xiv
English, as "hub" language, 101
Entropy, 11
  Boltzmann and, 14, 15–17
  computational ability of matter
    and, 177
  information and, ix, xx, 14–16,
    176
  information-rich anomalies
    and, 31
  multiplicity-of-states definition,
    16–24
  second law of thermodynamics
    and, 27
  Shannon and, 14–15, 17–18
  solids and, 176, 177
  statistical-physics definition,
    16–17
  steady-state of out-of-
    equilibrium systems
    minimizes, 32, 175
Entropy barrier, 40
Equilibrium, order emerging from
  out-of-equilibrium systems,
  29–30
Ernst & Young, 113
Ethiopia, 161
Evolution
  coevolution of markets and
    standards, 100

of information and economic
order, xix–xx
of physical order, 175–181
Experiential learning, 79–80, 81
Exploitation narrative, developing
countries and, 55, 58–59, 60
Export diversity, economic
complexity and, 157–161,
180
Exports
as crystallized imagination,
51–55
diversity of physical and human
capital and, 154–156
geographic distribution of
industries and, 131–134
knowledge and knowhow
embodied in, 52–55
Export structure, product space
and, 137–139

Facebook, 92
Familial societies, 115
Family networks
formation of, 115–116
low-trust familial societies and,
121–123
trust and, 121–122
Faraday, Michael, 59, 60, 69
Fijitsu, 92
Firmbytes, 89, 107
Firm interactions, social networks
and, 93
Firms
networks of, 89, 92–93
size of, 89, 91
transaction cost theory of,
89–91, 93
Firm-to-firm links
classification of, 94–95
collaborations or large projects
and, 102–103

cost of, 91, 93, 94–95
sizes of, 93–94
Ford, Henry, 60, 88, 171
Fordlandia, 170–171
Ford Motor Company, 87–88, 89,
170–171
France, government role in
economy, 122–123
Fruit exports, 155
Fukuyama, Francis, 109, 115, 116,
117, 121–122, 122–123, 179
Functions, order and, 63

Gaua Islanders, 170
GDP (gross domestic product), 146
GDP (gross domestic product) per
capita, export diversity and,
157–161, 180
Gene analogy, 142
Genetic factors, ability to
accumulate knowledge and,
84
Genotypes/phenotypes analogy,
130, 136
Geographic distribution
of industries, 131–136
of knowledge and knowhow, 77,
80–81, 127–128
of production of complex *vs.*
simpler products, 77, 83,
134–136
Germany, formation of large
networks in, 115, 116
Getting a Job (Granovetter),
112–113
Gibbs, J. Willard, 28
Gorilla Glass screen, 92
Governance, social capital and, 151
Government
bureaucratic burden and, 103
role in French economy,
122–123

Granovetter, Mark, 109, 111,
    112–113, 114–115, 179
Graphical user interfaces, 120, 142
Guardiola, Josep "Pep," 73–74
Guitar, augmentation of our
    capacities and, 66–67
Guns, Germs, and Steel (Diamond),
    169–170

Haber, Fritz, 58
Hadza people, 117
Hanaman, Franjo, 59
Hartley, Ralph, xvii
Hayek, Friedrich, xiv
Health care sector, costs as
    overbureaucratized network,
    104, 106
Heisenberg, Werner, 39
Helmholtz, Hermann von, 28
Hemingway, Ernest, 70
Herr, Hugh, 50–51, 61, 178
Hidalgo, Iris, 3–4
High-trust societies, 115, 120–121,
    122, 123
Homophily, formation of social
    networks and, 114
Honduras, exports, 132
HP (Hewlett-Packard), 142
Human capital, 148–149, 152
    export data and diversity of,
    154–156
Humans
    augmentation of capacities,
    66–67
    computational capacity of
    matter and, 178, 179–180
    as embodiment of knowledge
    and knowhow, 8
The Human Use of Human Beings
    (Wiener), 70–71

IBM, 95
Ideas, knowledge/knowhow *vs.*,
    61–62
Imagination, crystallized. *See*
    Crystallized imagination
Incentives, as production stimulus,
    77–78
India, economic growth in, 159
Individual limits on accumulation
    of knowledge and knowhow,
    79–81, 82, 83–85, 179, 180
Indonesia, 161
Industrial development/
    diversification, personbyte
    theory and, 139, 142–144
Industrial structure and size, trust
    and, 115–116
Industries, geographic distribution
    of, 130–132
Industry-location matrices,
    nestedness of, 132–136, 139,
    142–143
Industry space, 139, 141
Information
    ability to process, 35–37
    behind chaos, 30–31
    Boltzmann and, xiii
    computation of, 23–24
    conceptual aspects of, xv–xvi
    connection with knowhow,
    165–169
    contained in tweet, 13–14
    decoding, 23
    in DNA, 5, 22–23, 34, 166–168,
    176
    embedded in objects, 5–6, 8,
    11–13, 43–44, 45, 178
    embedded in solids, 33–35, 176
    embodied in product, source of,
    62–63

emerging from out-of-equilibrium systems, 28–33, 35, 175

energy and, 175, 177

entropy and, 14–15

environmental conditions conducive to growth of, 176–177

evolution of, xix–xx

irreversibility of time and, 26

mathematical study of, xiii–xiv

meaning *vs.*, xvi–xvii

physical nature of, xvii–xxi

as physical order, xv, xix, 5, 7–8

physical origins of, 28–35

sciences and, xiv

Shannon's theory of, xv–xvii, 13–15, 17–18, 19–20

social sciences and, xiv–xv

as something and about something, 7

"stickiness" of, 31–35

Information growth

computational ability of matter and, 35–37, 41, 176, 177–178, 181

computational capacity as constraint on, 75

economy as system of, 8–9, 177–180

entropy and, ix, xx

history of universe and humans and, xviii–xix

nineteenth-century physics and, 26–28

Information processing, as purpose of life, 43–44

Information-rich states, 18–24

properties of, 22–23

Information-rich steady states, out-of-equilibrium systems and, 29–31

Information theorists (cyberneticists), xiv

Information theory, xv–xvi

Innovative economic sectors, adaptability of firms and, 124

Instantaneous nature of reality, 40

Institutions

new institutional economics, 89–91, 93, 117–118, 123

social networks and, 44–45

See also Social institutions

Intel, 92, 95

International trade, product exports as crystallized imagination, 51–55

Internet, 92

iPads, 50

iPhones, 50, 92

iPods, 92

Irreversibility of time, in statistical system, 37–40

Italy, familial networks in, 122

Ito, Joi, 73

James, LeBron, 130

Jamestown colony, 170

Japan, formation of large networks in, 115, 116

Jet engine production, 154–155

Jigsaw puzzle analogy, 135–136

Jobs, social networks and, 112–114

Jobs, Steve, 65, 92, 119–120, 142

Joule, James, 60

Just, Sándor, 59

Kauffman, Stuart, 37

Kingston, 92
Knowhow, xviii
  connection with information,
    165–169
  as constraint on spread of
    economic development,
    169–171
  crystals of imagination and, 61
  defined, 6–7, 165
  embedded in networks, in
    economies, 167–169
  embodied in biological
    organisms, 166–168
  embodied in products, 52–55,
    65–71
  geographic distribution of, 77,
    80–81, 127–128
  information processing and,
    35–36
  objects and, 8, 41
  physical embodiment of, 73–74
  quantization of, 73–75, 87–88
  social isolation and loss of,
    169–171
  value of, 61–62
Knowledge, xviii
  accumulation of, 79–85
  creation of complex products
    and, 78–79
  crystals of imagination and, 61
  defined, 6
  difficulty of accumulating in
    networks, 106–108
  embodied in human networks,
    179–180
  embodied in products, 52–55,
    78–79
  genetic factors modulating
    ability to accumulate, 84
  geographic distribution of, 77,
    80–81, 127–128
  human capital and, 152

industrial development and
    accumulation of, 139, 142
  objects and, 8, 41
  physical embodiment of, 73–74
  products and practical use of,
    65–71
  quantization of, 87–88
  sharing practical uses of, 69–70
  tacit, 78
  value of, 61–62
  volumes contained in
    manufacturing networks,
    105, 106–107
  See also Personbytes
Korea, balance of trade with Chile,
    52, 54–55
Kuznets, Simon, 146–147, 149

Labor, economic growth and, 146
Labor markets, social networks
    and, 112–114, 121, 124
Landry, Dave, 139
Language, cost of interactions and,
    100–101
Latin America, familial societies in,
    115, 122
Law of induction, 59, 69
Learning
  experiential, 79–80, 81
  social nature of, 80–81
Leontief, Wassily, 147, 148, 155,
    162
Life
  ability to compute and, 37
  non-equilibrium systems and,
    32–33
  purpose of, 43–44
Light bulb, invention of, 59
Lovelace, Ada, 49, 69
Low-trust familial societies, family
    networks and, 120, 121–123
Lyell, Charles, 27

Mach, Ernst, xii
Machinarium, 92
Malaysia, export structure of, 137–139, 140
Managed by the Markets (Davis), 101
Mankiw, Gregory, 148
Manufacturing,, migration from United States to China, 161–162
Manufacturing networks
  Barbie doll, 101–102
  as dominant model of production, 105
  exchange of intermediate products in, 105–106
  personal computer, 92, 105
  volumes of knowledge and knowhow in, 105
Market interactions, cost of, 95, 100
  language and, 100–101
Markets, coevolution of standards with, 100
Mathematical study of information, xiii–xiv
The Mathematical Theory of Communication (Shannon & Weaver), xv–xvi
Matter, computational capacities of, 35–37, 41, 176, 177–178, 181
Maxwell, James C., 28, 69
Meaning, information *vs.*, xvi–xvii
Medicinal pills, context and value of, 63–64
Melanesians, 170
Message, minimum volume of data needed to specify, xvii, 13–15
Microsoft, 95
Microstates, entropy and, 16, 17

Minsky, Marvin, 7
MIT Media Lab, 52, 61, 62, 73
Mozart, Wolfgang, 84, 124
Multiplicity of a state, entropy and, 16–17
Music
  genetic factors in musical ability, 84
  instruments and access to knowledge, 66–67

National Bureau of Economic Research, 113
Natural sciences, xviii
"The Nature of the Firm" (Coase), 90
NEC, 95
Negroponte, Nicholas, 61–62
Nestedness of industry-location matrices, 132–136, 139, 142–143
Netgear, 92
Netherlands, exports, 132
Networks
  accumulation of knowledge and knowhow in, 106–108
  complex computation and, 179
  limits on ability to form, 74–75
  personbytes accumulated in, 88–89
  transferral of productive, 143
  transition points in structures of, 107
  See also Firms; Manufacturing networks; Professional networks; Social networks
Network size, familial societies *vs.* high-trust societies and, 115–116
Networks of firms, 92–93
  social capital and, 152
New institutional economics, 89–91, 117, 123

Newton, Isaac, 25, 40
New York Times (newspaper), 92, 113
Nicolis, 32–33
Nigeria, 161
Non-equilibrium systems
    life and, 32–33
    steady state of, 29–30
Nonequilibrium thermodynamics, 28
Nonspecific recurrent transactions, 94
Nortel, 95
Nova Lima (Brazil), 139, 141
Nyquist, Harry, xvii

Object-oriented programming, 120, 142
Objects
    as crystallized imagination, 44, 178–180
    information embedded in, 5–6, 8, 11–13, 43–44, 45, 178
    knowledge and knowhow and, 41
    See also Products; Solids
Observatory of Economic Complexity, 52
Occasional and specific transactions, 94
On Competition (Porter), 147–148
Optogenetics, 51, 61
Order
    emerging in out-of-equilibrium systems, 29–30
    functions and, 63
    growth of, 26–28
    See also Physical order
Ordered states, entropy and, 17–19, 21
Out-of-equilibrium systems
    computation and, 37

information emerging from, 175
information-rich steady states and, 29–31

Page, Jimmy, 70
Pakistan, economic complexity of, 157–159
Palo Alto Research Center (Xerox PARC), 119–120, 142
Panel Study of Income Dynamics, 113
Past, unreachableness of, 40
Personal computer
    production by network of firms, 92, 105
    professional networks and, 119–120
Personbytes, 83–84, 107, 180
    accumulated in networks, 88–89
    available in large networks with bureaucratic burden, 103–104
    defined, 82
    industrial development/ diversification and, 139, 142–144
    migration of manufacturing and, 161–162
    required to produce cars, 88
    ubiquity of products and nestedness of industry-location matrices, 135
Phenotypes/genotypes analogy, 130–131, 136
Physical capital, 152
    export data and diversity of, 154–156
    measuring, 153–154
Physical embodiment of knowledge and knowhow, 73–74. *See also* Objects; Products; Solids

Physical nature of information, xvii–xxi
Physical order
  evolution of, 175–181
  information as, xv, xix, 5, 7–8
  origins of, xii–xiii
  singularity of, on Earth, x
Ping-pong ball analogy, 37–39
Pirsig, Robert M., 49
Plant, Arnold, 90
Plymouth colony, 170
PNY, 92
Polanyi, Michael, 78
Polar Eskimos, 170
Political preference, genetic factors in, 84
Polynesians, 170
Porter, Michael, 147–148
Powell, Walter, 79
Prigogine, Ilya, 25, 28, 30–33, 37, 40, 175
Productive networks, transferral of, 143
Products
  apples vs. Apples, 49–50
  characterization of economies and, 155–156
  communication vs., 67–68
  economic value of and context of, 63–64
  geographic distribution of production of simpler and complex, 134–136
  importance of source of information embodied in, 62–63
  practical use of knowledge/knowhow and, 65–71
  stimuli for production of, 77–78
  See also Complex products; Objects; Solids
Product space, 136–139, 143

Product ubiquity, economic complexity and, 156–157
Professional networks
  social networks and composition of, 123–124
  social networks and formation of, 114–117
  trust and, 119–121
Proteins, information embedded in, 34, 176
Putnam, Robert, 121, 122, 135, 179

Quantization of knowhow, 73–75
Quantization of knowledge and knowhow, 87–88
Quantization principle, economies and, 168
Quantum Corporation, 92
Quantum mechanics, xiii

Raw materials, exploitation narrative and, 55, 58–59, 60
Real estate market, secondary to social network, 109–111
Reality, instantaneous nature of, 40
Ricardo, David, 148
River Rouge complex (Ford Motor Company), 87–88, 89, 105
RNA, embodiment of information in, 5
Roanoke colony, 170
Robotic limbs, 50–51, 61, 178
Rocket development, 143
Rolfe, John, 170
Romer, David, 148
Romer, Paul, 148
Route 128 (Boston), contrasted with Silicon Valley, 118–120, 124
Rubik's cube, 21–22, 23
Ruiz, Israel, 73
Russia, 60

Salter, Arthur, 90
Saltpeter exports, 55, 58
Samsung, 92
Saxenian, AnnaLee, 118–119
Scale economies, 87–88
Schrödinger, Erwin, 33, 34, 176
Seagate, 92
Second law of thermodynamics, 27
Seed, information and knowhow
 contained in, 166–167
Shannon, Claude, 9
 entropy and, 14–15, 17–18
 theory of information, xiv, xv–
  xvii, 13–15, 17–18, 19–20
Shared social foci, formation of
 social networks and, 114
Shipping costs, cost of market
 interactions and, 95
Shoes, information in form of, 45
Silicon Valley
 contrasted with Route 128
  (Boston), 118–120, 124
 personbytes of knowledge and
  knowhow in, 142
Simoes, Alex, 52, 139
Simon, Herbert, xv
Simpler products, production in
 most countries, 134–136
Singapore, economic complexity of,
 157–159
Smith, Adam, 87, 146, 148
Social capital, 149–151, 152
 measuring, 149–150, 153
 theory of, 111
 trust and access to, 121
Social context, of information
 growth, 43
Social group isolation, loss of
 knowhow and, 169–171
Social institutions
 familial *vs.* high-trust, 115,
  120–123

within-country variation in,
 118–120
Social learning, 80–81
Social networks
 adaptability of firms and
  networks of firms and,
  118–120, 124
 difficulty in forming, 83
 economic relevance of,
  111–124
 firm interactions within, 93
 formation of, 114–117
 formation of professional
  networks and, 123–124
 information exchange and, 44,
  45, 46
 knowledge and knowhow
  trapped in, 78–79
 labor market and, 112–114, 121,
  124
 market forces and, 111
 real estate market secondary to,
  109–111
 social capital and, 150–151
 trust and, 119–121, 123
Social sciences, xviii
 information and, xiv–xv
Society
 familial *vs.* high-trust, 115,
  120–123
 products that augment human
  capacity and complexity of,
  70–71
Sokolovska, Anna, 3
Solids, information embedded in,
 33–35, 176, 181. *See also*
  Objects; Products
Solow, Robert, 146, 147, 148, 149
Specific and recurrent transactions,
 94
Stadium example, ordered states
 and, 16–21

Standards
  coevolution of markets with, 100
  cost of market interactions and, 95, 100
Static steady state, 28–29
Statistical system, irreversibility of time in, 37–40
Steady state
  of non-equilibrium system, 29–31
  origin of information and, 28–30
Stock, diversity *vs.*, 152–154, 162
Study of Disadvantaged Youth, 113

Tacit knowledge, knowhow and, 78, 80
Tasmanians, 169–170
Teams, physical embodiment of knowledge/knowhow in, 73–74
Technological transfer, 143
Technologies, social networks and, 11
Tesla, Nikola, 59, 60, 62, 69
TFP. *See* Total factor productivity (TFP)
Theory of dissipative structures, 28
Theory of social capital, 111
Thermodynamic potentials, 31–32
Thermodynamics of the universe, 25–41
Thoreau, Henry David, 43
Time, irreversibility of, 25–26
  in statistical system, 37–40
Time travel, birth as, 3–5
Toothpaste, access to practical use of creativity and, 65–66
Torres Islanders, 170
Toshiba, 92
Total factor productivity (TFP), 147

TP-Link, 92
Transaction cost theory, 89–91, 93, 123
  economic sociology and, 117–118
  trust and reduction of, 117–118
Transition points
  breaks in knowhow carrying capacity of networks and, 167–168
  in structures of networks, 107
Travel, cost of market interactions and rates of, 95, 96–99
Tree, information processing by, 35–36
Triadic closure, formation of social networks and, 114
Trust, 109, 111
  developed *vs.* developing countries and, 124
  familial networks and, 121–123
  formation of large networks and, 116–117, 118
  formation of large social networks and, 123
  formation of professional networks and, 115–117
  reduction of transaction costs and, 117–118
  social networks and, 119–121, 123
Trust (Fukuyama), 115
Turing, Alan, xiv
Tweet, information contained in, 13–14
Twitter, 13–14, 92, 101

Uncertainty principle, 39
United Nations, bureaucratic burden and, 103
United States
  formation of large networks in, 115, 116

United States (*continued*)
  migration of manufacturing to
    China from, 161–162
Universe
  both frozen and dynamic, 35
  organization of, xii, xviii, 30–31
  thermodynamics of, 25–41
University of Notre Dame, 109

Value, of knowledge and knowhow,
    61–62
Venezuela, 60
Vidal, Marc, 110
von Braun, Wernher, 143
von Neumann, John, 14–15

Watt, James, 60, 146
Wealth
  augmentation of human
    capacity and, 68–69

economic development *vs.*,
    60–61
Weaver, Warren, xiv, xv–xvi
Weill, David, 148
Westinghouse, George, 59
What Is Life? (Schrödinger), 33, 34,
    176
Whirlpools, 29–30, 31, 32, 34, 175
White-collar workers, social
    networks and access to
    employment, 112–113
Wiener, Norbert, xiv, 70–71
Wikipedia, 101
Williamson, Oliver, 93–94, 102,
    106, 108, 118
World of Goo, 92
Wozniak, Steve, 142

Xerox PARC, 119–120, 142

César Hidalgo leads the Macro Connections group at the MIT Media Lab where he is also an Associate Professor of Media Arts and Sciences. He lives in Cambridge, Massachusetts, with his wife Anna and their daughter Iris.